5/21   SH 6-
                            scan

speed
dating[sm]

HarperResource

an imprint of **harpercollins***publishers*

YAACOV & SUE DEYO

speed
dating^{sm}

the smarter,
faster way to
lasting love

FIRST EDITION

Designed by Claire Vaccaro

Library of Congress Cataloging-in-Publication Data
Deyo, Yaacov.
Speeddating : the smarter, faster way to lasting love / Yaacov Deyo and Sue Deyo.
p. cm.
Includes bibliographical references.
ISBN 0-06-621255-3
1. Dating (Social customs)—Popular works. I. Deyo, Sue. II. Title.

HQ801 .D49   2002
646.7'7—dc21   2001039800

02   03   04   05   06   **QW**   10   9   8   7   6   5   4   3   2   1

To the couple who introduced us—Dick and Bev Horowitz

contents

contents

acknowledgments

Sue and I would like to thank the following people for their contributions to this book and/or to SpeedDating events. Without their help, this book would not have been possible.

Rabbi Noach and Rebbetzin Denah Weinberg, Rabbi Yitzchak Berkovits, and Rebbetzin Tziporah Heller for teaching us the Torah principles upon which the events and this book are based.

The five other founders of SpeedDating events who responded to my invitation to assist the Jewish people: Antony Beilinsohn, C. Casper Casparian, Dalia Laitin, Elliot Semmelman, and Tally Shashoua Aka Kosh. It was their dedication as volunteers that led to a system that has helped thousands of people and has started a new industry of round-robin dating.

Rina Hirsch for giving Elliot Semmelman the opportunity to participate in a dating program that gave Elliot the inspiration to come up with the raw idea of seven-minute, round-robin dating.

acknowledgments

Our agent, Daniel Greenberg, for suggesting we write a book about the principles of SpeedDating. Our editor, Toni Sciarra, for shaping our ideas into a book.

Rabbi Yitz Greenman, Adam Leiberman, Danny Moskowitz, and Michelle Chandler—they took a great, local idea with legs and made it into a worldwide phenomenon. Melanie Rosenkranz for all her behind the scenes research and her continuing management of SpeedDating International.

A sincere thank you to Rabbi Aryeh Markman, a man who has selflessly given me the encouragement and resources to try new projects—including SpeedDating. We thank the Los Angeles Aish HaTorah Branch, its students, supporters, and all SpeedDating branches.

To Dick and Bev Horowitz, Rabbi Nachum Braverman, Rabbi Twerski, Judy and Irwin Katsof, Uriela Obst, Rabbi Noach Orlowek, Ross Hirschmann, Marc Firestone, Chana Kalsmith, Rabbi Kelemen, Alan and Bonnie Cohen, Alan Gould, Meggy Ozyel, Jack McConaghy, Joel Mandel, Layne Dicker, Nancy Rose, Ken Fields, and Nora Cain. All of these individuals made invaluable contributions to the events and/or this book.

We especially would like to thank our parents for all their years of love and support.

A special thanks goes to E.W.D.—you know who you are!

I would like to thank my wife. I have held her in awe since we met. She is that which millions of voices over thousands of years have extolled—a valorous woman. She finished her part of this book while lying in a hospital bed for five straight months, caring for our unborn daughter Avigial. Both mother and daughter are now fine, thank you.

Finally, we thank God for the opportunity to write this book, for the blessing of meeting and marrying each other, and for everything we have received in life, both the revealed and concealed good.

"For to God is the whole earth and its fullness."

—Rabbi Yaacov Deyo
September 2001

speeddating—a smarter, faster way to lasting love

For someone seeking a meaningful and lasting relationship, today's dating scene can be brutal. You meet someone, begin dating, date more seriously, fall into a semi or full-time living-together arrangement—and then it doesn't work out, leaving one or both of you heartbroken. Often intensifying the pain is the "time factor": nine months, a year, two years, or more may have passed, without bringing you any closer to the goal of finding the right person for a committed relationship.

Now, that's not to deny that every relationship, successful or not, has the potential to be a profound learning experience and to increase wisdom. However, there's a myth in our society that getting to know someone well enough to make a commitment takes years, and that the only way to mature and learn who we are and what we want in a relationship is through these painful multi-year cycles of unsuccessful dating. To quote composer Hector Berlioz, "Time is a great teacher but unfortunately it kills all its pupils." Fortunately, relying on time and failed relationships is not the only path.

*SpeedDating*SM offers a smarter and faster way to date to find a lifelong relationship. Given the proper tools—such as knowing which questions to ask before the dating process begins and as the relationship unfolds—you can quickly and more confidently assess a relationship. While there's certainly no way around the work involved in evaluating a relationship and making it successful, the amount of time it takes to determine if a relationship is right and the amount of pain in the dating process can be minimized significantly. The phrase "Work smarter, not harder"—or more precisely, "Date smarter, not longer"—can be applied.

There's no way to predict that a relationship will last forever, but the SpeedDating approach will increase your certainty tremendously. Today fewer than half of marriages work out, so a typical couple could assume with reasonable accuracy that the probability of their relationship lasting is about 50 percent. The very confident may estimate their chances at 60–70 percent. In a school environment those percentages range from a C– to an F—from barely passing to failure! With SpeedDating you will know with significantly greater certainty that the relationship you choose to commit to will last. In addition you'll be much less likely to fall victim to a doomed relationship and waste precious time.

Sue and I wrote this book because the SpeedDating approach works. SpeedDating is for anyone seeking a lifelong

partner—whether you have been dating for years, are just starting out, or haven't dated in a while. These pages are filled with
stories of singles★ serious about finding a meaningful relationship with the potential to last their lifetime, yet frustrated with
and often burned by the traditional dating paradigm. You'll
learn how they incorporated the principles of SpeedDating
into their life, changed their approach to dating, and found the
relationship they were seeking. It has been a privilege and joy
to work with these and other singles, watching them escape the
pain and confusion of traditional dating and achieve empower-
ment and clarity. It is even more joyful to hear their success
stories when they find the right relationship.

a brief history of speeddating

SpeedDating began with a letter I wrote to my students in Los
Angeles. In the context of working to address Jewish continu-
ity, I invited them to my house to discuss ways to address Jewish intermarriage. After a number of meetings, we focused our
attention on trying to make Jewish dating more appealing and
user-friendly. From these discussions came SpeedDating
events, a unique form of round-robin dating in which each
person has seven seven-minute dates in one evening.

★All names have been changed and circumstances modified in order to protect the privacy of the people involved.

These dates are unique not only in duration but also in content. For example, in order to help singles get to know each other faster, SpeedDating mandates that in each seven-minute date, the daters cannot ask questions that can lead to snap judgments about the other person—"What do you do for a living?" "Where do you live?" or "What kind of car do you drive?" Everyone knows you can be a great lawyer but a lousy person. This restriction requires SpeedDaters to think about something more interesting to talk about! This process alone can be very revealing.

Within a year of the first SpeedDating event, SpeedDating events grew from a few a month in Los Angeles to weekly events in twenty-five cities worldwide. We believe the popularity of SpeedDating events comes in large part because of the underlying principles on which the rules of SpeedDating were built. For a complete list of the rules of the seven-minute SpeedDating events, look in Appendix A.

beyond the first seven minutes

This book expands on these core SpeedDating principles and offers additional dating tools and tactics that allow singles to more effectively evaluate a relationship before a large investment in time and emotions has been made. It provides the questions to ask yourself, your date, and others to make a more informed decision in the shortest amount of time with the maximum dignity and minimal risk of heartache.

While SpeedDating evolved from discussions with my students about the need for a more efficient approach to dating, its underlying principles are rooted in the Jewish tradition, passed down from generation to generation for thousands of years. In fact the Talmud, an ancient Jewish law book, suggests a method of dating that enables both parties to screen out unlikely candidates. Prior to developing SpeedDating, I incorporated many of these principles in the classes I taught. In fact, Sue and I used them when we dated each other—and if we hadn't, we probably would never have recognized each other as soul mates. We'll share our story with you in Questions 2 and 9.

In the ten years I have been teaching these fundamental ideas, many hundreds of people have improved their lives and their relationship skills by incorporating these principles into their lives. Sue and I have witnessed over a hundred people meet their special person and embark on a committed relationship with confidence that the love would last. Among these students, we know of only a handful of divorces. The success my students and I have had using these principles inspired Sue and me to incorporate them into the SpeedDating events, my classes, and this book.

This book is divided into two sections. Part 1 provides essential questions to ask yourself as you prepare to date. Through these questions we introduce key SpeedDating concepts that will enable you to date more effectively. Part 2 provides the questions you need to ask yourself and your date in order to relatively quickly assess whether the relationship has the potential to last. In addition, this section addresses the pace of dating. When I teach SpeedDating principles, students often ask when in the dating process they should ask certain questions. We have found that people differ vastly in the pace of dating that is comfortable for them. The Pacing Questions in Part 2 act as a guide if you have not yet found your own pace, or if you suspect that the pace at which you date is interfering with your success in finding a meaningful relationship.

While SpeedDating is based on the tenets of Jewish philosophy and wisdom, it can be applied universally regardless of religion. We invite you to explore in this book what thousands have already discovered. SpeedDating is the new way to date, evaluate a relationship, and even marry.

—RABBI YAACOV DEYO

speed
dating ^{sm}

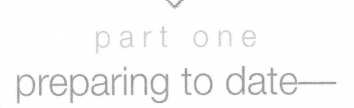

preparing to date—

Essential Questions to Ask Yourself before You Begin Dating or Commit to a Relationship

Each question in Part 1 explains a key dating principle that will help you date more effectively. This section clarifies some common misperceptions about dating and enables you to better understand the type of person with whom you will be able to form a lifelong relationship.

Since knowledge only becomes wisdom when it is applied, we've provided an exercise at the end of some of the questions. By taking a few minutes to complete each exercise, you will begin the process of applying the SpeedDating principles and making them your own.

Let's begin!

question 1

what is my desired outcome?

 The first step to SpeedDating is consciously committing to finding a lifelong, meaningful relationship—and not settling for less. If you ask many people if they're thinking of a long-term commitment with the person they're dating, they'll say, "No, no, we're just dating." You meet them three years later, and they're saying the same thing. For the SpeedDating process to work, dating must be seen as a vehicle for achieving a long-lasting, committed relationship.

But couldn't we assume that almost anyone reading this book is looking for a meaningful, lasting relationship? Certainly, yes. Yet you may be dating in ways that have little chance of success. You may be falling victim to relationships that seem headed in the right direction, but in fact are not. We like to say that these relationships craft half of a lifelong relationship—the long part! These long-term faux relationships are common time-wasters and heartbreakers because they typically last eight months to three years, but never hold the potential for lifelong commitment.

Let's examine a few such scenarios to help identify and avoid them in the future.

the shaper

Shapers try to change the person they're dating into someone he is not in order to make the relationship work. When Shapers encounter a deal-breaker situation in a relationship, they believe that if just given enough time and persuasion, the other person will change.

Jane is a classic Shaper. When we met Jane, she was dating John. Jane admired John's intelligence, sense of humor, and strong work ethic. She believed they were perfect for each other. There was just one problem—John's consuming passion for sports car racing. When he wasn't working, John spent the majority of his time devoted to his hobby—either at the race-track or at home working on one of his many cars. Jane disliked everything about this hobby. Cars didn't interest her, and she especially hated going to the track, where her emotions ranged from bored to terrified.

She figured that John would outgrow this hobby someday.

She certainly couldn't imagine marrying someone who spent his life devoted to car racing. She bought John a tennis racket and lessons at the local health club. When he didn't develop an interest in tennis, she bought them both mountain bikes and would regularly suggest that they go for bike rides. For over eighteen months Jane tried to pull John away from his passion, with no success. Instead of recognizing and dealing with this deal-breaker situation, Jane continued to try to change reality.

There's nothing wrong with exposing a potential partner to areas of your life to see if he too will be interested, but it's unhealthy and unrealistic to try to mold a person into something he is not.

Had Jane been SpeedDating, she would have handled the situation differently. When she discovered that John, as wonderful as he was, was essentially married to a hobby she despised, she would first look within herself to see if in fact it was a deal breaker. If it was, she would have explored for a limited time the possibility that he might be open to expanding his interests beyond car racing. Once she saw that he had no desire to do this, and if it was a true deal breaker, she would have accepted that reality and broken off the relationship.

Whenever we suggest this approach to a Shaper, the immediate question asked is, But what if he changes after we break up? Our answer: He probably won't. If he does, you can reevaluate and perhaps restart the relationship. But holding on to the fantasy of him changing carries a great price: time, heartache, and—for women who want to have children with a committed partner—fertility.

The trap Shapers fall into is the mistaken belief that either they or time have the power to change someone. Many Shapers hold on to their fantasies because they lack confidence that they will meet someone as "great" as their current boyfriend. The reality is that while the Shaper is desperately holding on to a relationship destined for failure, Mr. Right may be passing, undetected, through her life.

The Shaper's mistake can be tragic. A while ago, Sue met a woman who had just broken up with her boyfriend of eight years. From the first month they began dating, he told her he would never get married. She heard him, but she didn't believe him. For eight years she believed he would change. He didn't. At age thirty-six she finally broke up with him. If her goal had not been marriage, this might not be a tragedy. But her dream was always to get married. She was convinced that this man was the one, and she spent nearly a decade of her life thinking that some day he too would realize this. While of course at thirty-six this woman's life is far from over, and she can certainly still meet her soul mate, this level of heartache leaves emotional scars that are difficult to recover from and may affect future relationships.

Shapers are typically women. It is well known in traditional Jewish circles that women have a special ability to understand men (especially their significant others) and exert influence over them. This special ability is called *bina*. The negative side of this quality of *bina* is that women sometimes come to believe they can change someone who is not open to change—and hence a Shaper is born.

Men also fall into faux relationships, but what they typically do is avoid focusing on the potential deal-breaking issue by ignoring it. Which brings us to our next faux relationship scenario.

the avoider

Avoiders, similar to Shapers, sense that major issues lurk in their relationships. However, unlike Shapers, they choose not to focus on these. Typically an Avoider is enjoying some aspect of the relationship, and by ignoring any potential deal breakers, he can continue the relationship for the short term. Once he no longer needs the relationship or a better one comes along, he breaks it off.

Tom worked at a start-up company. He was fresh out of business school, cash-poor but loaded with options. While pursuing the frenetic start-up lifestyle, he met Caitlin. Caitlin was twenty-three, she had grown up in Beverly Hills and by the age of seventeen knew what she wanted: to get married and raise her family in Beverly Hills near her parents. Family was her top priority, and she could not imagine working outside of the home after she had children. Tom had moved to Los Angeles from Utah. Both his parents had worked when he was a child. He began working at age twelve to help his parents with the finances. One of his main goals was to save enough money so that he could start his own company.

Tom and Caitlin called us shortly after moving in together. One Sunday we met in our living room, and after pleasantries, Caitlin blurted out, "He wants to charge me rent!" The room became a little tense. Tom began to fidget while Caitlin stared at Yaacov, expecting an answer. Clearly we had a war-crime-level situation. Kidding aside, Caitlin's dismay at Tom's insistence that she contribute to the rent underscored an issue Tom had been avoiding for months.

Caitlin and Tom had been dating for ten months. Caitlin was ready to commit to marriage, but Tom was unsure. When Yaacov had spoken with Tom previously, he had said he just needed more time. But after ten months of dating, Tom needed more clarity—not time. Yaacov asked Tom if there were issues about Caitlin he felt unsure of. Hesitant at first, he explained, "Caitlin would be a great mother—she really loves children." However, he believed they had conflicting goals. He felt strongly that Caitlin should help him achieve his goal of starting his own company by age forty, and he sensed that she felt just as strongly about not working after she had children, which would prohibit her from contributing to the family income. They had never discussed the issue because Tom felt awkward bringing it up, and he didn't want to rock the boat—he liked Caitlin and enjoyed being with her. So he rationalized that more time would lead eventually to clarity.

Stories like Tom's are common and are accepted as normal. People date for months or even years under the assumption that time will bring the insights they need to decide whether to move forward or end the relationship. While clarity can come with time, it often does not—especially with Avoiders. During seven-minute SpeedDating events we ask participants to decide at the end of the seven-minute date whether they want to date the person again. The commitment and closure is good training for Avoiders.

Tom was behaving like a classic Avoider. Deep down he had known for months that Caitlin's dream of being a stay-at-home mom was not one he could help her achieve, but he had ignored this issue. Tom was new to L.A., and he was lonely. He cared for Caitlin and enjoyed his life with her, but he just couldn't envision them getting married.

When we pointed out to Tom that he was not being fair to Caitlin by avoiding the troubling issues—that in effect he was stringing her along for his benefit—he could see it. He realized that if he did not clarify his position in the relationship, he would be hurting and using his girlfriend. Tom perceived himself as a good guy and wanted no part of hurting someone else, especially someone he had formed an intimate relationship with.

Had Yaacov not challenged Tom, he and Caitlin might have dated for years, making no progress on clarifying and resolving Tom's uncertainties. Instead, Tom and Caitlin were open to the idea of learning about the SpeedDating approach to help them expedite the decision-making process.

That Sunday afternoon Yaacov helped Tom express the concern he had been avoiding. He admitted to Caitlin that there was a potentially serious issue preventing him from committing to her. Within the next couple of weeks Tom and

Caitlin learned more about themselves and the potential for their relationship than they had in the previous ten months. They learned that their value systems were too disparate to reach a compromise, and they decided to break up.

If Tom and Caitlin had been SpeedDating from the beginning, Tom would have brought up the deal breakers much earlier, even though he would have had to give up the benefits of the relationship sooner than he would have liked. And Caitlin would have been more assertive in determining whether Tom shared her value of stay-at-home parenting. This doesn't mean that she would grill him about this issue on the first date! There's a pace to dating—which we'll discuss in detail in Part 2—but she certainly would have clarified this crucial deal maker/deal breaker within the first three months of dating.

defaulters

Another common mistake is to fall into what we term a "default relationship." These occur because people mistakenly believe the myth in our society that you must completely enmesh yourself in a relationship to obtain the insights and information you need to make a commitment.

This myth is very dangerous because it clouds the point at which the "dating" stops and a "relationship" begins. By the time Defaulters figure out that the relationship is not right, they are so enmeshed with and invested in each other, they either feel an obligation to continue the relationship or they don't have the strength of character to leave it.

When Paul and Ann began dating, there was an immediate attraction. Paul was a struggling actor, and Ann was a physician's assistant. Within a couple of weeks they were seeing each other almost every day, and within a few months they were fully entrenched in each other's lives. A couple of years later Ann began suggesting they get married. By this time Paul felt an obligation to marry Ann because she had been supporting his acting career for the past year. Intuitively, however, he sensed that they were not right for each other. He'd had this sense for the past year and a half—but being with her was so convenient, he kept procrastinating. They did end up getting married, having a couple of children, and then divorcing. Paul confided to us that as he walked down the aisle at his wedding, he sensed Ann and he would end up divorced.

While this story is extreme, the point is clear: Paul and Ann began a serious relationship before they had decided that they were right for each other. The extent of Ann's giving to Paul was well out of proportion to the commitment Paul had made to her, and Paul never made the conscious decision of wanting to be in a relationship with Ann—it just happened.

Properly understood, dating is the due diligence a person should perform to decide if he or she wants a relationship with another person; *dating is not the relationship.*

SpeedDaters date with one goal in mind—to gather the

information and insights they need to make a decision about whether to commit. SpeedDaters use the SpeedDating tools to collect this information, instead of enmeshing their lives with another before a commitment to the relationship has been made.

the cynic

The Cynic consciously or subconsciously no longer believes that she can find a lasting relationship. In fact, many Cynics believe that lifelong relationships are mere fantasy. Unfortunately, the Cynic is usually the product of too many failed relationships.

Carol, at age forty-five, still dreamed of finding a committed relationship. However, she had known from the start of her past two relationships that they would never last. Her current boyfriend, Don, was fun to be around but had serious lapses in responsibility. He had filed for bankruptcy, still had debts, and had no plans to change his free-spending behavior. Carol knew she would never even lend him money, let alone believe the relationship had any real prospect of commitment.

When Carol attended a SpeedDating seminar, she was shocked to realize that if she followed SpeedDating principles, she would not have dated her previous boyfriend, nor the man she was seeing now. "And if I hadn't dated them, then I wouldn't have had a relationship for over six years!" she said with horror.

Implicit in her statement is the classic Cynic's assumption that these short-term relationships, or "companionship relationships," as we call them, are better than risking being alone, holding out for the right relationship. On a certain level, Cynics don't believe that a third option exists—that there is a better relationship out there and that they can find it.

Choosing the short-term companionship of a relationship void of any hope of lifelong commitment isn't necessarily wrong, but it is not SpeedDating. If your goal is a relationship that lasts, cynical thoughts, comments, and actions won't bring you any closer to your goal. If you see patterns of the Cynic within yourself, remember that the SpeedDating process has worked for people of all ages and stages.

Contrast Carol the Cynic with Marni. Marni learned the principles of SpeedDating at age thirty-three. She committed to not settling for anything less than a meaningful relationship she believed would endure. For five years she found no one— that's five years of not dating anyone longer than three or four months. Then, at age thirty-eight, she found her Mr. Right. Today she is married, and they recently had a baby girl. While it took Marni a while to find the right relationship, by age thirty-eight she had found what she was seeking, while Carol, at forty-five, was still searching and doubting.

What do the Shaper, Avoider, Defaulter, and Cynic have in common? They do not focus on their true goal of finding the *right* relationship, not just *any* relationship. SpeedDating does not mean getting into just any relationship faster; it's finding the right relationship faster and ending the dating phase of your life forever.

If you don't consciously decide upon a desired outcome before and during dating, you risk falling victim to one of the time-wasting relationships outlined above. SpeedDating is about making conscious choices on your own behalf.

how can i tell when i'm in love? and how do i know the love will last?

When we ask singles how they can tell when they're in love, virtually all answer confidently. When we ask how they can tell they are in a love that will last, the responses become much less confident.

We're going to give you a practical guide for determining when you're in a love that will last. Also, we will provide clues as to why you may have been misled about finding lasting love in the past.

chemistry

There is an aspect of love that cannot be expressed verbally. It is the aspect based solely on feelings and intuition, which by definition are indefinable. It is this emotional aspect of love that most people identify with being in love.

When we ask singles, "How can you tell when you're in love?" the vast majority respond by saying something like:

- I have strong feelings and intuition, so I just know.
- I think about the person all the time.
- I feel excited, with a tingling sensation.
- I can't imagine not seeing the person again; I want us to spend every minute together.

While a powerful emotional pull is certainly one component of love, relying on it alone means that people walk around thinking that love is like the New England weather: it comes and goes capriciously. And because of this capriciousness, they'll always hedge their bets—bring a raincoat even on a sunny day. For many, that means playing it safe, maintaining an exit strategy, and not committing.

If love is a feeling that mysteriously appears and disappears, how can we ever be certain that it won't suddenly disappear? How will we ever trust that the person who loves us today will love us forever? How can we be sure that the person we love today will be the person we love tomorrow, or in ten years?

So, what do people do? They date for eight months, and ask, "Are we still in love? Better wait a bit longer." They date another year and ask, "Are we still in love? Better wait a bit longer." They date for another two years. . . .

In truth, dating is a series of educated guesses, and we can never know with 100 percent accuracy if a relationship will last. But if we believe that love is grounded only in feelings, there can never be *any* assurance that the person we're in love with today is the person we will love tomorrow. It is a sad reality in this society that when we see a couple "in love," we assume one of two things—that they're not married, or that they're newly married. In other words, we recognize that this feeling doesn't last for most people—which is true when the relationship is based only on those feelings.

SpeedDating brings clarity and hope to this issue by emphasizing a second aspect of love in lasting relationships. This aspect is based not on feelings and intuition, but on knowledge and the intellect. In an ideal relationship, both partners can articulate *why* they are attracted to each other.

knowledge

The Bible says, "Adam knew his wife, Eve." This is not just a euphemistic expression for physical intimacy. On a deeper level, it means that he truly knew who she was and loved who she was. Their relationship was based on a mutual understanding of each other's virtues.

Without knowledge, without using your intellect to get to know who you are dating, you run the risk of either getting into a relationship doomed to failure or overlooking what could be the perfect relationship.

One example of rushing into a relationship without knowledge of the other person we call the Shooting Star relationship. In a Shooting Star relationship, the couple has an immediate attraction to one another, assumes the relationship is meant to be, invests their heart and soul in the relationship, and then discovers, once they get to know each other, that the relationship doesn't have a future.

We met Eric when Sue invited a few of her graduate school classmates to our house for dinner. Eric was about twenty-seven at the time, and very friendly, outgoing, and positive. About six months later he began dating Beth. Like Eric, Beth was an avid fitness buff, and in fact had been an Olympic gymnast. Almost immediately Eric was telling us that he was in love. "I really think I want to marry her," he told us. "I can't stop thinking about her, and I want to be with her all the time. The feeling between us is so intense, it's amazing!"

When we asked Eric to describe Beth, he couldn't describe anything about her beyond superficialities such as her love of sports and cats and that she seemed to be indescribably sweet. His "love" for her was strictly this feeling, this amazing energy surge he felt when he was around her. But he did not yet know who she really was. His heart was telling him he loved her before his mind had a chance to analyze the relationship.

We believe people generally rely only on their feelings to gauge the potential of a relationship because many of us are trained from birth to evaluate relationships solely on feelings of attraction. We grow up on fairy tales like Cinderella and Snow White. At the most impressionable of ages we learn from these stories that "love" is rooted almost exclusively in a feeling, a certain chemistry or connection. Why the Prince falls in love with Cinderella or Snow White, and not another, is a mystery. All he knows is that Cinderella can dance and has small feet. With Snow White, the Prince knew even less, since he fell in love with her while she was sleeping! In this paradigm there is no way to prepare to meet the right person, since the intellect plays no role.

While the SpeedDating approach holds that mutual attraction is critical to a relationship, it also incorporates vital input from the intellect. You *can* have control over your love life when you use both head and heart.

Returning to our story of Eric and Beth—within a few months of Eric telling Yaacov that he was in love with Beth, the relationship ended. When we saw Eric after the breakup he looked exhausted. He confided that Beth turned out not to be a nice person. During one of their dinner dates, Eric witnessed Beth giving her phone number to another man when she thought Eric had gone to the car to get her coat. When he confronted her about this, she told him that she couldn't say no to the guy, but she certainly wouldn't date him. Eric later learned that Beth was going out with other men while they were dating, even though they had agreed to date exclusively. He understood that her Olympic training in combination with her parents' pressuring her to compete had ingrained in her the desire and need to always be the center of attention. He also recognized that it wasn't healthy to be involved with someone like this. He was crushed, "I really loved her!" he told us.

This is the classic Shooting Star pattern—jumping into a relationship before the intellect has a chance to provide input. Eric is as bright as they come, but like many people, his emotions outpace his intellect. When Eric met Beth, his feelings of attraction registered much more quickly than the time it would take his intellect to gather information about her as a person.

Investing heavily in a relationship before truly knowing the other person wastes time and breaks hearts. Feelings of attraction are beautiful and something to look for. But this love is incomplete by itself. Without knowing the person and being able to articulate specific reasons for loving that person, the relationship may not endure. While it starts out flying high, it risks falling fast—like a shooting star.

Often students ask us, "But what about 'love at first sight'?" Yes, there are many cases of people meeting each other for the first time and intuitively knowing that this is the right person—and their intuition turns out to be right! However, intuition is often wrong—or simply a biological attraction, as with Eric. So, SpeedDaters acknowledge their feelings, but continue the due diligence process of using their intellect to learn who the other person is before investing in the relationship.

There is another mistake that can be made by relying too heavily on emotional feedback. We call it the Buried Treasure relationship.

Many people believe that if they don't have intense feelings at the start of a relationship, the relationship holds no promise. This destructive myth has probably kept many potential couples from forming beautiful relationships. In fact, were it not for knowing the principles upon which SpeedDating is based, we (Yaacov and Sue) may never have married!

In the middle of his rabbinical studies, Yaacov came to Los Angeles as an intern. Sue was in Los Angeles about to begin a graduate program in business administration. Sue's initial impression of Yaacov was not exactly positive! At the urging of a mutual friend, Yaacov and Sue had agreed to meet at a local synagogue to discuss some questions Sue had about Judaism. As Sue waited for Yaacov outside the synagogue, she heard a loud crash. Someone driving an old Volvo had been making a left at the intersection nearby and had run into a car going straight. Sue ran to the intersection, and getting out of the Volvo, looking dazed, was Yaacov! When the police arrived, Yaacov began to tell them that the accident was his fault. "NO, no!" said Sue. "He doesn't mean that—the other car may have run a red light." "Sorry, ma'am," replied the officer, noting Yaacov's response in his little spiral book, "he has already confessed."

"You don't do that in L.A.!" exclaimed Sue after the officer left. "You can get sued now—you should have left this to an attorney." "But I think the light was yellow," said Yaacov. Sue was stunned. Honesty was one thing, but she knew Yaacov wasn't 100 percent sure the accident was his fault—and to confess to a police officer in a city known for ambulance-chasing attorneys was unthinkable! While Sue appreciated and admired Yaacov's dedication to honesty and his integrity, she concluded (inaccurately, we both add!!) that Yaacov was a bit naive and belonged back in yeshiva behind his law books, protected from the "real" world.

Throughout Yaacov's internship in Los Angeles, Sue and Yaacov saw each other around the synagogue quite frequently, and Sue's impression of Yaacov remained the same. Fortunately, Sue and Yaacov met again a year later. Sue, being aware of the principles behind SpeedDating, was open to meeting Yaacov again because she did appreciate his honesty and integrity, even though she didn't feel that special "chemistry" for him. Sure enough, Sue's feelings for Yaacov changed as they got to know each other.

In our experience, about 30 percent of relationships actually begin with no strong feelings of connection or attraction. Two people meet and intellectually recognize that they share mutual respect and admiration, though the relationship lacks a certain emotional component that they are seeking. In these Buried Treasure relationships, the potential for the relationship is strong, but the couple's feelings for each other are temporarily hidden. If you find yourself in a situation in which you admire your date, but don't "feel" for him, don't be so quick to drop him. There's a limit to the amount of time to give to such a relationship, because it could be that the relationship doesn't have chemistry and never will. But it's possible you simply need time with the person, helping him achieve his goals and vice versa, for the spark of the relationship to ignite.

knowledge plus empathy

In our experience, feeling chemistry for and having knowledge of the other person still doesn't mean you're in love or that the love you feel will last. Each person also needs to identify with the other's goals to the extent that they begin giving to each other, helping one another accomplish their goals. We'll discuss this further in later questions.

To summarize, a key to SpeedDating is realizing that lasting love has both emotional and intellectual components. A relationship based only on feelings is destined to burn out, and a relationship based only on intellectual connection without the spark of attraction cannot ignite.

SpeedDating Exercise

The next time you are dating someone and believe you might be in love, complete the following checklist to assist you in determining whether it has the potential to last.

How Can I Tell When I'm in a Lasting Love Checklist

1. I can articulate four (nonphysical) virtues about the person that I respect, and can give examples of each.

2. As my date discusses her goals and dreams, I feel interested and truly motivated to help her attain them—or at least I can be encouraging.

3. I am concerned that his or her goals be accomplished.

4. I feel a special connection and attraction—a chemistry.

Note: For a more complete checklist, see page 169 in "Conclusion: Is This My Soul Mate?"

question 3

am i attracted to who people are or to what they have or what they can do for me?

 In Question 2 we discussed how to tell when you're in love. But then the question arises, in love with whom? In order to ensure that your love will last, you need to love the person, not things peripheral to the person. In other words, are you zeroing in on external attributes—such as his car, job, clothes, waist size, table manners, or house? Or are you trying to find someone whose core being you admire—qualities such as his positive attitude, kindness, loyalty, responsibility, and so on—so that regardless of the external situations you find him in later in life, you will still love and respect him?

If you choose to focus on external circumstances, you risk that when the circumstances change—and they usually do—

the foundation of your relationship will be lost. However, if you find someone you truly admire, then you can be confident that the love will last.

The difference between what a person has and who he is can be confusing because it is not uncommon for a person's possessions and life circumstances to reflect his core self. However, this is not always the case—so we can never rely on external attributes to define a person. We must look beyond the superficial. This certainly doesn't mean you must uncover the very depths of a person's soul while dating! That's not necessary and probably not possible. All you need to do is gain an understanding of the person's core character traits and direction in life. In this question we'll define character traits, and in Question 4 we'll explore life direction, goals, and values. In Part 2 we'll discuss how to determine these aspects of a person without having to spend years together or deeply enmesh your lives.

Character traits influence how a person views and responds to the circumstances and situations he is in. They generally exist independently of life circumstances. Examples include patience, impatience, positive attitude toward life, easiness to anger, mellowness, kindness, selfishness, drive, and laziness, to name a few. A true character trait is consistent: a happy person is generally happy regardless of circumstances. Of course a happy person can feel sadness, but someone with a happy character will tend to view a sad situation in the most positive, constructive light and try to make the best of it.

Chart A	Chart B
CHARACTER TRAITS (SAMPLE)	EXTERNAL CIRCUMSTANCES (SAMPLE)
Positive outlook on life	Career
Sensitive	Education
Giving	Successful business
Kind	Expensive car
Outgoing	House ownership
Reserved	Physical condition
Patient	Attractiveness
Laid-back attitude	Wealth
Ambitious	Poverty
Honest	
Generous	
Loyal	

A friend of ours, Sarah, *is* happy. At one point in her life she was dating a man she admired and hoped to marry. He, however, did not feel ready to commit and broke off the relationship. Sarah felt genuinely sad and disappointed by the news, but she didn't fall into despair or lose hope of finding her soul mate. Within a reasonable time she responded constructively by calling her support group and positively reframing the experience: if she was not meant to be with this person, there must be an even better person out there. Sarah's positive personality is like a ball floating in a pool. The news of the breakup pushed her down, but she popped back to the surface quickly.

To distinguish between who someone is and what they have, ask yourself, Could this aspect of this person be taken away by time, or by someone else? In the case of career status, money, looks, and possessions, the answer is yes. In the case of character traits such as honesty, positive attitude, and kindness, the answer is no.

It is surprising to some to realize that qualities like intelligence and athletic ability are not character traits. Although they are something a person is born with and typically don't change, they don't reflect a person's character. It's perfectly acceptable to desire a person who has a certain external circumstance, like intelligence, but that can't be all you are looking for—a brilliant person can be kind, a brilliant person can be cruel. As Victor Frankl discusses in *Man's Search for Meaning,* the one thing—the only thing—we ultimately always have is the freedom to control how we respond to our circumstances. The nature of our responses, how we choose to respond to these circumstances, makes up our character.

In Question 2 we met Eric, the graduate student who fell in love with Beth, the former Olympic gymnast. When he first told us that he was in love, we asked him what he loved about Beth. He listed the following:

- We both love to exercise.
- She's so cute.
- I feel great when I'm around her.

Let's look at these in light of what you've just read about character traits:

- "We both love to exercise." This is a shared interest. A shared interest can be a positive sign, but an interest is not a character trait. And one shared interest is not enough evidence that a relationship will last, especially if you don't yet know the person's character.

- "She's so cute." Attraction is important in a relationship—but it's not a character trait. Attraction can be a positive sign, but if you don't really know who the person is, that attraction may be fleeting.

- "I feel great when I'm around her." Eric's feeling great around Beth could have been a sign of the intuitive love we discussed in Question 2. But intuition can be wrong, and in this case Eric's was. Once Eric discovered Beth's character, he no longer felt attracted to her; in fact, he was disgusted by her self-centeredness.

Bottom line: what Eric "loved" about Beth was what she could do for him—make him feel great and keep him company while he exercised. This is "selfish love." Unlike selfish love, true love doesn't hinge on what people have or on what they can do for you.

selfish love

In her book *The Magic Touch*, Gila Manolson relates a popular story in Jewish tradition about a young man who sat down to eat a freshly cooked chicken. He turned to his teacher and said, "I love chicken!" The teacher laughed and answered, "If you truly loved chicken you would care for them—not kill and eat them. What you love is yourself—and what you love about the chicken is what it can do for you."

Tragically, many people approach dating and relationships the same way. They think, What can this person give to me? instead of What can I give to this person? They look for someone who can respond to and meet their needs, and what they end up loving about their boyfriend or girlfriend is what that person does for them, not who the person is. In other words, they love the circumstances that person is in, rather than the person. The tragedy about this type of love is that when the circumstances change, the love is gone. One way to avoid this tragedy is to be sure that you can articulate specific character traits you love about your partner and that he can articulate core traits in you that he loves.

Sally came to talk with Sue because she was tired of getting her heart broken. Sally was a beautiful woman who had spent over seven years as a successful professional dancer. Her pattern in relationships was that she would meet a man, they would begin dating, and fairly quickly the man would tell her that he loved her and hint that he wanted to marry her. Some of the men saw her dance before they met her and professed their love even before the first date! All too often, Sally would invest her heart and soul in the relationship, only to find that within a few months, the boyfriend would end the relationship, leaving her heartbroken and feeling used.

After learning about the concept of selfish love, Sally understood that when these men told her that they were "in love," they were actually in love with themselves and how great they felt being seen with someone as beautiful as Sally. They weren't in love with Sally—how could they be? They didn't know her! And in truth who Sally was as a person was not important to them. The next time a date told Sally that he loved her, she asked him, "Really? What specifically about me do you love?" The man paused, thinking, and then said, "You're beautiful." "That is an aspect of me that will change over time as I get older," Sally replied. "Is there anything else?" Her date was startled. "I mean," he stammered, "you're a beautiful person." "Thank you," said Sally. "What specifically have you seen me do or heard me say that leads you to believe this?" Never again was Sally's heart a victim of selfish love.

Another tragedy of selfish love is that it can last for years—even decades—and show itself for what it is only when circumstances change. It leads to many divorces later in life. When Carol met Bill, he was a successful businessman earning about a quarter of a million dollars a year. When asked what she loved about Bill, Carol talked about how smart a businessman he was, what a great car he drove, and how well he played tennis. Within a year of dating they became engaged and got married. About five years into their marriage, Bill's business began to falter. There was a strong possibility that the business would go bankrupt, taking with it Bill's entire fortune. Fortunately the business survived and began to prosper again. During the hardship Carol confessed to Yaacov that if the business did go under, she would divorce her husband: "I can't stay married to someone who is broke—that's just not something I signed up for when I got married."

Now, before jumping to the conclusion that Carol is a shallow, selfish person, know that she gives about 5 percent of her income to charity a year, volunteers for Meals on Wheels, actively takes care of her aging parents, and is raising her children with a strong sense of self-esteem. Carol has many good qualities, but she confused selfish love with true love. She had married Bill for all that he could do for her, rather than for who he was as a person.

Finally, we want to mention a subtle form of selfish love. It involves loving how someone's character traits benefit you, but not liking how these traits emerge in other situations. For example, Yaacov is extremely generous (Sue wrote this part!). Even in the early years of our marriage when finances were extremely tight, he would think of ways to give to Sue that

cost little or no money. Years later, after we were out of graduate school, Yaacov began to give huge gifts to financially
struggling newlyweds—things like brand-new refrigerators and
couches! Initially Sue was very upset. How could he be giving
away such expensive gifts when we had enormous student
loans and no pension plan? But then Sue realized that this was
another expression of Yaacov's innate generosity, and her love
for him grew! Once Sue was able to appreciate that Yaacov's
generosity was an important, enduring quality of his character,
we were able to discuss our financial constraints and agree on a
compromise: Yaacov has a budgeted amount he gives away,
and Sue is confident of our ability to repay the student loans
and save responsibly.

Identifying the Right Person, Even If He Is in the Wrong Circumstance

Sometimes you have to dig a little to see a person's true character traits. How often is it assumed that a doctor must be
responsible, an attorney a crook, a fat person lazy, a wealthy
person smart, and a poor person irresponsible? External attributes can blind us to someone's true character, even in the face
of abundant evidence to the contrary. The key is to know the
character traits you're looking for, so you can see beyond your
date's circumstances to discover who he is as a person.

Jennifer, a SpeedDater, prioritized the top four character
traits she wanted in a lifetime partner: a strong sense of respon-

sibility, sensitivity, loyalty (willingness to commit to a long-term relationship), and a positive attitude. When she met Paul, he was a struggling writer in Los Angeles living in a studio apartment and watching every dime. He had graduated from a top college three years before they met, and during those three years had experienced some minor success as a writer.

Before learning about the principles of SpeedDating, Jennifer would not have considered Paul a candidate for lasting love because he was pursuing a risky career and was not established financially. However, by understanding the difference between a temporary situation and a character trait, Jennifer could see beyond Paul's current circumstances to who he was as a person.

As they dated, Jennifer learned that Paul had the character traits she was seeking. She could see that he was financially responsible, and she loved his positive attitude toward life and his sensitive nature. It didn't matter to Jennifer how Paul was going to earn a living; she knew that he wanted to provide for his family and that he'd be capable of supporting a family even if his writing career didn't work out.

Jennifer also could tell that Paul loved her. He could articulate aspects of her character that he deeply admired and respected, such as her sense of humor and her commitment to helping others—from trying to set up two people on a date to buying flowers for a sick friend.

Within six months of dating, Jennifer and Paul became engaged. Their financial life was not easy at first. However, Jennifer had enough evidence of Paul's commitment to financial responsibility that she encouraged him to pursue his dream for at least another year. Within eighteen months of their marriage, Paul was hired as a writer on a popular TV show. But the story doesn't end here. After two years on that show—and a month after Jennifer and Paul had their first child—Paul was fired. Jennifer was certainly concerned about finances, but she had confidence that Paul would either find another writing job or move on to something else. Within six months, Paul had another job working for a different major studio on another top TV show. Today Paul is a producer in Hollywood, and he and Jennifer have a beautiful, healthy marriage. They were able to maintain their relationship through the tough financial times because their relationship was based on mutual respect and admiration of each other's character, not superficialities that could easily change. They truly loved each other.

To sum up: appreciating someone's core character traits is a key ingredient to lasting love. Shared life direction and goals—or at least a respect for each other's life direction—and chemistry are also necessary. Here is an equation to keep in mind:

Chemistry + knowledge & respect for core character traits + empathy and identification with his or her goals = strong potential for lasting love

SpeedDating Exercise

1. List all the character traits you admire in others. If there are specific circumstances you hope your partner will have, such as a good job or car, think about the character traits that would lead someone to those external circumstances.

2. Now assume you will only be allowed to have four of the character traits in a partner. Choose the four you believe are most important.

Note: It is not uncommon for singles to be accused of being too picky. How many good character traits do you expect another person to have? If you have trouble narrowing down your list to four, it's possible you're being too picky. Remember that no one is perfect, including you.

Another way to determine whether you are being too picky is to reflect on the character traits of people you've dated. If you've dated many people who have the character traits you seek, but you keep finding reasons not to commit to the relationships, then you might be too picky.

It's important to maintain a healthy selectivity in dating, but if you find that you are exhibiting signs of being too picky and are feeling trapped in this behavior, you may want to seek the help of a qualified counselor or therapist.

question 4

what do we have in common—and does it matter?

 Countless relationships have begun because the couple discovered early on that they had "something in common." However, many of these relationships are doomed to fail from the beginning. The question is not, Do we have something in common? It is, *What* do we have in common? Some interests you may share with another person have no relevance to the success of the relationship, yet it is vital that you share others. Knowing the difference is the key in SpeedDating.

In general, relationships have a greater chance for success if the couple's shared interests and ideas are of great importance and deeply felt by both people, as in the case of life goals and values. Common minor interests or hobbies generally will not affect the health of a relationship either way—for example, if politics are not of great importance to either couple, then even if they have opposing political views, the health of their relationship won't be impaired.

In the chart below we've diagrammed the aspects of commonality (or admiration and respect) you should seek in order of importance, from the inner circle outward.

key aspects of personality

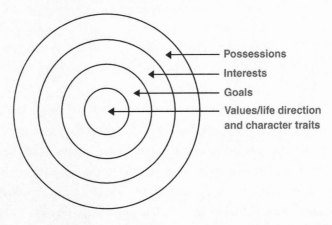

Possessions
Interests
Goals
Values/life direction and character traits

The most important, generally, is the inner core—a person's values and life direction, plus character traits that we spoke about in the previous Question. Next in importance are goals—how the person plans to achieve the life direction he's chosen. After that comes interests—like golfing or traveling.

And finally, possessions. Possessions can be what a person owns or what a person was born with, such as intelligence, artistic ability, or good looks. We don't mean to say that possessions are not important—it may be very important to you to marry someone who has a good sense of humor. But the key is not to say only that you want a humorous person—but that you want a person who is funny *and* who shares certain goals or values.

That's why a critical ingredient to the SpeedDating process is understanding what is important to you so you can look for that in another person—or at least determine that what is important to you will be respected by your partner.

Typically this process involves having a sense of your priorities and life goals. It seems obvious, yet many daters miss this point: without clarifying what's important to you and where you're headed in life, it's virtually impossible to recognize who you will be able to love long-term. The process of getting to know ourselves is lifelong, so if we waited until we were absolutely certain about who we are at the deepest of levels, we might never be able to commit to a relationship. Still, all of us have a sense, or can develop a sense, of our priorities.

Nina was a successful businesswoman, traveling the world restructuring companies in financial distress. While she knew she wanted a long-term relationship, she had struggled for years with the questions of whether or not she wanted to marry and have children. Her parents had divorced when she was ten, causing her severe trauma. Later she witnessed how her parents essentially forgot her grandparents when her grandparents entered a home for the aged. "Why should I get married?" she would reason. "Half of those who marry end up divorced. And why would I have children? They'll probably just abandon me when I'm old."

During her twenties Nina entered therapy to resolve some of these relationship issues. In addition, she sought out role models: couples with strong marriages and loving children. She even lived with one of these families for six months so she could witness healthy relationships in action. By her early thirties, she was beginning to have confidence that she would be able to sustain a marriage and be a parent, but she still wasn't sure she wanted to commit to such a life.

She continued to date, but didn't find anyone she wanted to marry. At one point she decided to take a three-week vacation instead of cashing in her vacation time for pay, as she usually did. She spent three weeks traveling around New Zealand. As she sat on a bench at Auckland University watching a father play with his two-year-old son, she became aware of an inner emptiness that her typically hectic life shielded. She knew then that she wanted to shift her focus. On the flight home she made a conscious decision to commit to finding a long-term relationship with someone who wanted to invest time in raising a family. When she returned to work, she inquired about positions at her company that would not require travel. Within six weeks she had transitioned to a new position.

About two months after returning from New Zealand, Nina attended a wedding. At the reception, a friend introduced her to John. They struck up a conversation, and Nina found herself telling John about her trip and how she had decided there were more important things in life than her career. John completely understood. When he had been in medical school, he had gone through a similar process of prioritization and had decided to become an emergency room doctor instead of a surgeon because he wanted more time for family, friends, and enjoying the outdoors.

Before Nina and John left the wedding reception, they exchanged e-mail addresses and phone numbers. Through e-mails, phone conversations, and many dinner dates, Nina and John realized that their initial connection was developing into something with great potential. Four months after meeting, they became engaged. Today they have two beautiful children, and Nina works part-time at her company.

Nina met her lifelong partner only after she understood where she wanted to go in life. Knowing this helped her recognize a potential partner and helped him recognize her. In addition, not only did Nina know where she wanted to go in life, but she took steps to make her goal a reality: she changed positions in her company. John had done the same in his choice of a medical speciality.

If Nina and John had met before Nina's epiphany in New Zealand, John would not have felt a connection with Nina because her values would have been much different from his. And Nina would not have appreciated John's laid-back work philosophy. "I would have thought John was a bit of a slacker," Nina admitted.

Most students with whom we work don't need years in therapy and a trip to New Zealand to clarify their priorities and life direction. However, many have never spent quality time thinking about these issues as they relate to a long-term relationship. Clarifying what you want from life is a core component of the SpeedDating process. And it is not uncommon for the singles we work with to take time to think about these issues.

Another practical reason for clarifying your life direction is that a committed relationship is not an end in itself. Imagine you get in a car with someone and ask them, "Where do you want to go?" and they answer, "I don't know; I just wanted to get in the car." This is analogous to the way many approach a relationship. They don't think about what they want to accomplish with the relationship, they just want a relationship.

Imagine the following scenarios:

Scenario A: A couple, Peter and Paula, meets and discovers that they both love watching kung fu movies. This shared interest creates a bond, and they begin a relationship. A month or so later they discover that they want different things out of life: Paula wants to be a doctor, which requires years of study and geographic flexibility; Peter wants to stay in his hometown, continue working as a mechanic, and start a family soon after marrying. Their different visions of where they want to go in life will create tension in the relationship—just as if two people in one car want to go in opposite directions. Yes, they could compromise, but it's much easier to compromise on what movie to watch than to sacrifice life goals.

Scenario B: Now imagine a different couple, David and Dorianne. Like Paula, Dorianne wants to go to medical school. David thinks that is a terrific goal. He's a graphic artist who loves to travel and can work almost anywhere. They both share the same life vision of eventually having a family, living in a rural mountainous location, and raising their children as Unitarians. In this scenario the relationship can help each achieve his and her personal and joint goals. When they look five to ten years down the road, they both see the same picture. The relationship is not an end in itself, but allows them to pursue their shared dream.

We're not saying that every interest and goal must be shared in order for the love to last, but if top-priority personal goals must be sacrificed or ignored for the relationship to work, resentments will eventually build, and the relationship becomes primed for conflict. As we discussed in Question 2, most people are striving for a meaningful love that will last. There is greater certainty that love will last and even grow if the couple shares a common direction in life, which usually includes having some similar priorities. That's why you need to have some sense as to where you want to go in life and what's important to you.

SpeedDating Exercise

1. Spend a few minutes right now writing down what is important to you in life. These can be anything: family, friends, career, kayaking, skiing, reading, watching movies, wine tasting, etc.

2. Now consider each item on the list and ask yourself:

- What is the value behind this interest or goal? Typically we have values that motivate us to seek a given direction in life. If we can identify these underlying values, we can look for people who share them. Even if a couple's interest or goals are different, if their values are the same, it's a strong sign that their love can last, as was the case with David and Dorianne.

- How important is this item to you? Is it something you can live without or something you must do or accomplish in life in order to feel you are being true to yourself and your dreams?

- How important is it that a potential partner share this interest or value? You may find that you have some very strong interests that your partner need not share so long as he or she supports them in you.

As an example, let's go back to Peter and Paula. After they broke up, Paula attended a SpeedDating seminar and performed this exercise:

paula

My interests and goals	What is the value behind this goal or interest?	Priority of interest/goal for Paula	Priority of interest/goal for partner
Medical school	I value helping people and being financially secure.	Very high priority for me—this is a life goal that I cannot sacrifice.	Partner must respect/admire this goal of mine—doesn't need to share goal of becoming a doctor.
Kung fu movies	I enjoy relaxing and value having time to relax.	Fun, but low priority; there are many ways I can relax besides watching kung fu movies.	Okay if partner doesn't share this interest, but I would like to be able to have fun with my partner.
Tennis	I value staying in shape for health reasons. Also, tennis helps me relax.	High priority—strong interest.	Would be great if partner shares this interest, but okay if not—but very important that he wants to stay in shape for health reasons.
Religion	I believe in God.	Medium priority now—but I want children to be raised with my religion, so it will be a high priority later in life.	Partner must share the same religious values.
To live on the East Coast near my family after medical training.	I value being with family.	High priority.	If partner strongly wants to live elsewhere, I could compromise.

Paula discovered that a low-priority interest—watching kung fu movies—was the basis of her initial attraction to Peter. To base a relationship only on a shared interest or two is risky, especially when the interest is of low priority—as Paula discovered.

Having a variety of shared interests and goals in a relationship is a little like diversifying your investment portfolio for more security and profit: the more interests, goals, and values you have in common, the greater the certainty your love will be permanent and will weather tough times. You need not have everything in common—it's unrealistic and even unhealthy to expect to find someone who loves everything you love and vice versa—but it's wise to look for someone who shares a similar life direction and common core values.

If you're struggling a bit to clarify your life direction, try asking yourself the following questions:

The future: Imagine your future and what you would like it to contain. This will help you understand what you most value and how you see yourself expressing those values.

- What are my dreams for the future?
- What dreams would I regret not fulfilling?
- How would I like to be remembered after I die?

The present: Now look at the present. Is what you're doing today aligned with your values, goals, and dreams? If not, then either you need to make some changes, or you don't truly have the values you stated above.

- What am I doing now?
- Will what I'm doing today help me achieve my goals for the future?
- Do I feel good about what I'm doing?
- Did I consciously choose to be doing this—and is this what I want to be doing in the future?

what type of person do i enjoy giving to?

 SpeedDating is not just about finding any relationship; it's about finding one that has the potential to endure. A strong sign that a relationship will last is that the couple enjoys giving to each other. When mutual, healthy giving is present in a relationship, the love in that relationship has the potential not only to last, but to grow stronger and deeper each year.

Not all types of giving build love. Typically when the idea of giving is introduced at SpeedDating seminars, students rush to express their frustration with relationships in which they "gave and gave and never got back." This frustration is usually a symptom that the wrong kind of giving is taking place.

thoughtful giving: love-building giving

There is only one form of giving that builds love between two people. In Hebrew it is called *chessed*. *Chessed*, or thoughtful giving, occurs when the giver's intention is primarily to help the recipient attain his or her goals *and* the recipient is open to receiving the help.

In the early stages of a relationship, thoughtful giving can be as simple as a man remembering that his date enjoys Italian food and offering to go to an Italian restaurant, even though it is not his first choice. Later in a relationship, as the couple knows each other better, it can take the form of the woman offering to spend a Sunday at the hardware store helping her contractor boyfriend pick out supplies, when this is not her ideal Sunday activity! Thoughtful giving builds love because it bonds people through a mutual commitment to helping one another achieve their goals.

Thoughtful giving is difficult to achieve if you don't respect the person's character or the direction he is taking in life. Imagine a woman who is determined to finish college, but whose boyfriend doesn't see the value of education. It would be difficult for him to give to her in a way that helps her achieve her goal of graduating, because he doesn't respect it. It doesn't mean that the boyfriend cannot give to her, but doing so in these circumstances is typically more challenging.

Thoughtful giving then requires that:

- You have some knowledge of the person. The more aware you are of who he is—his likes, dislikes, goals, and general direction in life—the richer the giving can be.
- You think about what the other person needs, and ask if you don't know.
- You assess whether the person is open to receiving your giving.
- You give or refrain from giving accordingly.

If your giving lacks any of these aspects, then you are giving in a way that won't build love, and you may be giving in an unhealthy way. Let's explore unhealthy giving so you can avoid it in the future.

unhealthy giving

Unhealthy giving can hurt the giver, the receiver, or both. Often in unhealthy giving situations, either the giver or the recipient becomes jaded and angry. Below are examples of unhealthy giving and its corrosive effects:

Giving with an Agenda

Giving with an agenda means that the giver's primary motivation in giving is to further his or her own goals. The gift may
be what the recipient needs, and the recipient may be open to
receiving it, but the main reason the giver is giving is for her
own benefit, not the recipient's. Typically this form of giving
builds resentment because the giver does not feel appreciated,
and the recipient does not feel genuinely cared for.

Carol thinks her boyfriend Bob dresses like a geek. It
embarrasses her, and she's convinced it's hurting his career. She
gives him a $250 gift certificate to Brooks Brothers and offers
to help him pick out his clothes. Let's say Carol is right: Bob
dresses like a geek, and it's hurting his career. And let's say he
is open to her help. While all this is very positive, this giving
will not build love between Carol and Bob if Carol's overrid-
ing motivation is to alleviate her embarrassment. On some
level Bob will sense the lack of thoughtful giving, and Carol
will have expectations that Bob should appreciate the gift,
even though the main reason she is giving is for herself.

Since upgrading Bob's wardrobe would help Bob, and he's
open to the help, Carol has a choice regarding her giving. If
when she honestly thinks about this situation she sees that the
gift is mostly to ease her embarrassment, she can choose to shift
her thinking—acknowledge that the gift is to herself and not
expect appreciation from Bob. In fact, *she* should be appreciative if he spends the gift certificate and he wears the new
clothes. If, however, she can honestly focus on how this is

helping Bob, and can learn not to be embarrassed if he doesn't wear the clothes, then she can be confident that she's involved in thoughtful giving that will bring the two of them closer.

Giving with an agenda is guaranteed to bring heartache and resentment to the giver when the giver hopes to get love in return. Mary wants to keep dating Sam. She buys gifts for Sam, tidies his apartment, runs errands for him, becomes physically intimate with him, all with the hope, i.e., the agenda, of making the relationship work. Often the Marys of the dating world believe that if they can just give enough, the person they are dating will love them or will learn to love them. This is a fundamental misunderstanding of what we call the physics of giving. The more Mary gives to Sam, the more she will feel invested in him. However, if he isn't giving back, then his investment in her and love for her will not increase. In fact, if a giver gives in an unhealthy manner, the recipient may become resentful and come to despise the giver because he feels conflicted about his obligation to be grateful. Realize now that if the person you are giving to does not show signs of wanting to commit to the relationship, no amount of your giving will change that person's mind.

Giving That Is Really Taking

Giving with an agenda can take a more insidious form. When the "giver" doesn't consider the recipient's needs or feelings at all and the "giving" is purely to further the giver's agenda, the action is no longer giving at all; it is taking. This is manipulation: it disguises taking in a giving package and hurts the recipient. Unlike the examples above in which Carol and Mary were motivated in part to help the recipient or the relationship, this type of "giver" may not care at all about the recipient or the relationship.

Mark buys Cheryl an expensive dinner and tells her he loves her, hoping that she will spend an intimate evening with him. Cheryl may mistake Mark's gestures for signs of a blossoming relationship. Manipulative giving can destroy people like Cheryl and Mark. The Cheryls of the world become bitter and cynical about ever finding meaningful love. The Marks of the world, unaware of the damage they are doing to themselves, often continue until they are incapable of forming a meaningful bond with another human being.

The SpeedDating approach can help the Cheryls of the world recognize the Marks of the world before damage has been done.

Giving to the Wrong Person

When singles find themselves giving in a healthy way, but the love in the relationship is not growing, it's often because they are giving to a "taker." There are two types of people in this world: givers and takers.

A giver looks upon life and thinks, How can I help my world become a better place? This world might be his family, his friends, or his community. It certainly will include working on himself to become a better person, who will in turn make the world a nicer place for the people around him. While givers are involved in acquiring possessions like homes and cars, their motivation for acquiring is consistent with their goal of giving: a home is purchased to provide an adequate and secure environment for themselves and their family; a car is purchased with similar motivations.

In contrast, a taker thinks, How can I acquire as much for myself as possible? Takers may mistakenly believe that if they can just acquire enough stuff, they'll be fulfilled. Takers are often labeled as selfish or egocentric. About a month after moving to Los Angeles, Yaacov saw a car with a bumper sticker that epitomized the taking mentality: "Whoever Dies with the Most Stuff Wins." The tragedy of the taker is that his goal is never realized—he is never fulfilled. A friend of Sue's worked at an investment house in which a main principal of the firm made $10 million in one year. Sue's friend asked this man what his goal was now that he had made so much money. His response: "To make $20 million next year!" A taker may use his money to set up a charitable fund and help his relatives, but his driving motivation in life is still to increase his acquisitions.

There are two reasons why the taker will never be satisfied. The first is that he desires a given object *because* it is beyond his reach. Once it is within his reach, it is no longer of any interest to him. It is difficult for a taker to form a lasting, meaningful relationship because once the person he desires is "his," he'll lose interest.

The second reason why a taker is never satisfied is based on

Jewish mysticism. The concept of ownership can be misleading. My car and my house are not my own the way my arm, my leg, and my thoughts are my own. A person can never unite with an outside item the way he is united with his body, his thoughts, or his soul. A car is not and never will be able to be part of a person's body or soul. If we try to expand our domain with things that cannot be a part of us, we will never accomplish our goal of expanding our true domain. Paradoxically, the soul is expanded through giving to others and becoming invested in them. The more a person thoughtfully gives, the greater his or her spiritual domain becomes, and the more fulfilled he feels.

Giving to a taker is extremely painful. A taker feels entitled to what he is given. He has strong expectations that those around him should give to him, so he shows them little if any appreciation. In addition, as a taker is focused on acquisition, it's difficult if not impossible for a taker to give thoughtfully.

As a note, there's a difference between a taker and a recipient. A taker is as we described above. A recipient is a giver who receives something from another. Unlike a taker, a recipient feels and shows sincere gratitude when given to. A recipient does not have an attitude of entitlement and appreciates the time and effort of the giver.

A key to lasting love is finding a giver to give to and becoming a giver yourself. Unfortunately, our society trains us to be takers. Many people become takers because they believe it is the way to attain success and fulfillment. We tell students that if they are dating a taker, they should not write off the person immediately, but should first expose the person to the idea of giving and see what happens. Quite often the taker realizes his error and changes perspective quickly. It's important, though, to know when to cut your losses with a taker.

Thoughtful giving in a relationship is like sunlight to a plant. Thoughtful giving between two givers nurtures the relationship and is strong insurance that a relationship will endure and grow forever.

SpeedDating Exercise

We recommend that you practice thoughtful giving by performing at least one small act of thoughtful giving each day. This giving can be to a family member, coworker, friend or acquaintance. Be sure to follow the steps for thoughtful giving:

1. Given what you know about the person, think about what he needs and wants.
2. Ask the person what she needs or wants, if you don't know.
3. Assess whether the person is open to receiving your act of giving.
4. Give or refrain from giving accordingly.

These acts of giving can be very small—such as noticing that someone at your office received a fax on the communal fax machine and bringing it to her, or remembering that your grandmother is lonely and calling her once a week.

question 6

am i reliving the same bad date over and over again?

 Often what prevents us from meeting the right person is a bad habit or an unhealthy pattern. Unhealthy patterns typically do one of two things—they either prevent us from recognizing the right person or prevent the right person from recognizing us. In this section we'll explore the ramifications of unhealthy patterns and how you can pull yourself out of those you may have.

There was a movie made a few years ago called *Groundhog Day*. This lighthearted romantic comedy actually portrayed a deep truth about life. The main character, Phil, played by Bill Murray, was desperately trying to attract a refined and kind woman named Rita, played by Andie MacDowell, but his obnoxious behavior and cynical approach to life were repulsive to her. In order for someone like Phil to attract someone like Rita, he would have to change his patterns of behavior. In the movie, Phil kept reliving the same day—Groundhog Day—over and over again until he was able to dislodge his old patterns of behavior and replace them with healthier ones. Before Phil truly changed, he tried all kinds of tricks and manipulations to win Rita. It was not until he had changed his egocentric character and come to truly care about other people that Rita became interested in him, and he was able to break the endless cycle of Groundhog Day.

This movie is a metaphor for our lives. In your own life you will keep reliving the same unhealthy patterns until you consciously and deliberately break them. If you're attracted to men who don't commit, you will continue to be attracted to men who don't commit until you consciously break that pattern. On a spiritual level, too, our experiences will repeat until we "get it right." The challenge is to become aware of the pattern and strategize ways to break it. In the movie, the need for change was clear; unfortunately, life is often not so clear or well scripted. Moreover, it's all too easy to rationalize these patterns or blame them on other people or on circumstances.

The good news for Phil in *Groundhog Day* was that time stood still as he broke his pattern. In the real world life does not wait for us to change—it keeps moving forward. It breaks our hearts when we meet men and women in their forties and even fifties who have been unable to find or maintain fulfilling relationships because of destructive patterns they have been repeating for twenty to thirty years!

However, once you do break an unhealthy habit, your life

can change dramatically! All of a sudden, new and different types of people walk into your life; the types of people you *want* to meet. Opportunities you never thought possible suddenly become realities.

Some people become so enmeshed in their destructive behavior that they come to believe that their pattern *is* reality. Since their pattern is causing events in their life to turn out a certain way over and over again, they conclude that this is the way life is—for everyone! Janice is attracted to men who don't commit. Over the course of ten years she has had her heart broken repeatedly by these men. After a while, she comes to believe that men don't commit—not just the men she is attracted to, but *all* men! Her resulting negativity and cynicism further prevent her from achieving her goal of finding a loving, committed relationship.

We do this as a society, too! The typical dating scene brings a lot of heartache. This heartache is seen as a normal and healthy part of maturing. Many times singles have said to us, "That relationship really broke my heart. I spent three years in it, but I learned a lot about myself and relationships." How tragic! Quite often they could have learned the same lessons without the pain by using SpeedDating principles. As a society, we have come to believe that our ineffective pattern of dating is the only way to date!

Let's take this one step further. This flawed dating paradigm often leads couples to believe they have found a lasting love when in fact they have not. That may be one reason why today's divorce rate exceeds 50 percent. As a society we come to believe that lasting relationships simply don't exist. Take a look at prime-time television. Sitcoms feature husbands and wives who are disgusted with each other, or singles on a constant, unsuccessful search for a long-term, committed relationship. We certainly aren't advocating a return to the repressive social structures of previous generations. Our point is simply that lasting love in which couples truly respect and love each other is real. It has existed throughout time, and you can create it in this generation. Negative patterns and beliefs will prevent you from reaching this goal.

For all these reasons, it's important to examine your previous dating experiences to see if you have any patterns that result in unhealthy or ineffective dating. If you are over thirty-five and still dating, chances are that you have some. It may be that once you become aware of your unhealthy patterns, you can break them. Awareness and desire can be powerful pattern-breakers. However, if you cannot stop the destructive behavior on your own or with the help of a friend or a date coach, you may want to seek the help of a qualified therapist or counselor.

We discussed some common unhealthy patterns of dating in Questions 1 and 2. Here are a few more:

pattern 1
LOOKING FOR PERFECTION

Many years ago a young man traveled a long distance to visit a wise man. The young man, in his thirties, was concerned because he had not yet found a wife. When he met the wise man, he asked for his blessing to find a wife. The wise man gave him a blessing and wished him well. A year later the young man returned. "You were here a year ago," said the wise man. "Yes," replied the young man, "but I am still single." "Why do you think this is so?" asked the wise man. The young man replied, "I have not yet found the woman who was made just for me." The wise man responded, "You are mistaken. She crossed your path many times, but you did not recognize her because you are looking for perfection! Marriage is about growth. When there are no rough edges, there is no possibility for genuine growth!"

Imperfection is inherent in all human beings. To look for the perfect person, or the person "just right for you," is to search for a fantasy and perhaps miss your opportunity to build a long-term meaningful relationship.

We find that sometimes this search for perfection stems from a person's conscious or subconscious lack of confidence in her ability to solve problems that may arise in a relationship. Since all relationships, including healthy ones, will have challenges, it's important to have confidence in your ability to make a relationship work.

This pattern may also be rooted in an attitude of entitlement. Some people simply believe they are entitled to a certain ideal man or woman, even though they themselves may be far from their own idea of perfection. We knew a forty-eight-year-old man who had never married because he said he was looking to marry someone with a model's figure. Ironically, this man was overweight and prematurely bald. His character was not refined, and he was struggling in his career. He didn't exactly fit his own requirements!

pattern 2
JUDGING SUPERFICIALLY

In Question 3 we discussed the dangers of judging someone based entirely on their external circumstances. During seven-minute SpeedDating events, we ask participants not to ask superficial or judgmental questions that can prevent them getting to know who someone really is, such as "What do you do for a living?" and "Where do you live?" Often people do not take the time to get to know their date before making snap judgements about him. We will discuss this in detail in Question 13, "Is This an Action, or My Interpretation of an Action?"

pattern 3
NOT TAKING RESPONSIBILITY—BLAMING OTHER PEOPLE AND CIRCUMSTANCES

Your character and life circumstances are made up of a combination of heredity and environmental factors. However, it is up to you to take responsibility for both. Taking responsibility for your life empowers you to create your own destiny. In addition, it is truly the only way to find happiness and success in life. Otherwise, you will always perceive yourself as a victim of circumstances who is unable to direct your life. While you may have faced barriers to meeting the right person, ask yourself, Now what? Are you going to blame others and your past for the rest of your life, or work to find a solution? It may be time to move on and take responsibility for finding the right person. It's not your parents' fault, regardless of what happened in your childhood! As an adult you have the choice of taking responsibility and making improvements, or choosing not to and remaining stuck in your present circumstances.

pattern 4
INABILITY TO COMMIT

A pattern we often see is the inability to commit to a relationship. Typically this problem afflicts men. Usually the root of this pattern is the person's belief that if he just waits a little longer, someone even better will walk into his life. If you are this type of person, this is what we have to say to you: there will *always* be someone more attractive, smarter, richer, or anything you want in your future. What else is out there? is not the question. The question goes back to Question 1 in this book, "What Is My Desired Outcome?" If your desired outcome is a lifelong relationship, that will only come by making a commitment to someone. If your desired outcome is to date the prettiest woman or the richest man, you will be hard-pressed ever to find or maintain a long-term relationship, because there will always remain the possibility of meeting someone more attractive or wealthier than the person you're dating now.

More than likely, however, if you are reading this book, your challenge is not committing—it's finding someone who wants to commit. Unfortunately, this is a significant challenge for many people we meet, and one we'll discuss in more detail in Part 2.

pattern 5
FEELING ATTRACTED TO UNHEALTHY PEOPLE

If you find that you have a pattern of being attracted to people who are irresponsible, abusive, addicted, or otherwise harmful to themselves or others, we strongly recommend you find a competent therapist to help you extricate yourself from this destructive behavior. It is well beyond the scope of this book and our training to counsel individuals in this area. In fact, we do not date-coach such people unless they are also seeing a trained counselor.

SpeedDating Exercise

If you suspect you may be enmeshed in an unhealthy pattern, try these exercises.

1. Rent the movie *Groundhog Day*. Imagine a script based on the same concept in which you are the main character. What is your Groundhog Day? What lessons do you need to learn to break your unhealthy cycle? What behaviors do you need to change?

2. List all your previous relationships. (We realize this may be a painful process, so try to be gentle but also objective.) For each relationship, ask yourself:

- "Why did this relationship begin?" Think about what attracted you to this person.
- "Why didn't this relationship work out?"

3. As you evaluate your relationships in this way, do any trends emerge? It may be that you have an assortment of unhealthy behaviors, but none is a pattern. As you become aware of the principles behind the Speed-Dating process and start putting them to use, you may begin to enjoy more effective dating.

4. Whether you see a pattern or not, ask a trusted friend or a counselor if she has ever identified any destructive patterns in you.

5. In Question 9 we'll discuss how to assemble a team to help you achieve your goal of finding a lifelong relationship. Be sure someone on the team can help you extricate yourself from the patterns you've discovered.

question 7

am i spending as much time in product development as i am in marketing?

 By now you should have a fairly solid image of the type of person you'd like to find for a committed relationship. In previous Questions you've asked yourself what type of character you are seeking, what life direction you want, and who you would enjoy giving to. So a tough question now to ask yourself is, Am I willing to become Ms. Right to attract Mr. Right? (or vice versa). We don't mean that you should change who you are, but that you can commit to a process of improvement, regardless of how great you already surely are.

Most companies have two main departments devoted to selling their products: marketing/sales and product development. The marketing/sales department's job is to inform the world about existing products and make them look and sound as good as possible through packaging and advertising. Product development takes the existing product, which is typically in good condition, and makes it even better. The best and largest companies in the world recognize the need for both.

People are not products, but there's something to be learned from this successful business model. Most singles are well aware of the need to market themselves and are busily doing so. Any effort to make the external self look as good as possible would be included in marketing—clothes, makeup, working out, hairstyle, good manners, and so on. The need for smart marketing should not be minimized. It's an important sign of self-esteem to want to look and behave attractively. Effort spent finding and going out on dates could be called sales. This, too, is an important and essential element in the process.

However, typically much more effort is expended on marketing/sales than on product development. Hence the question, Am I spending as much time in product development as I am in marketing? SpeedDaters spend at least as much time improving their character as they do marketing themselves to others.

Why is this question important? Because who we attract into our lives is directly correlated to who we are as people— our character and life direction. What we put out into the world is what comes back to us.

It's not unusual for us to meet people who fall woefully short of the standards they expect their future partners to meet. Many say that they have worked on themselves in the past and feel they are good enough or that they are happy with who they are and see no reason to change.

This reasoning is faulty; no matter how evolved a person has become, the reality is that you and your future partner will have differences! You need to have the flexibility to look honestly at yourself and change in response to these differences. In his book, *Men Are from Mars, Women Are from Venus,* John Gray gives example after example of how men and women experience and handle the same situation differently. The most refined man will not understand how to comfort his spouse if he does not understand how he and she are different. He will need to be open to changing how he responds to some situations. For example, when he is faced with a problem, a man's first reaction is usually to solve the problem, whereas a woman's first reaction is usually to process the feelings she experiences because of the problem. For a relationship to be healthy a man must be able to realize that his natural reaction will not work with his partner—and vice versa. Thus, the "willingness to improve" muscle must be strengthened in order for a relationship to work.

In Question 6 we discussed the movie *Groundhog Day.* Phil, played by Bill Murray, was the quintessential "all sales and marketing, no product development" guy. He manipulated people to get what he wanted. He considered most others beneath him, and he scorned them—often openly! He used women, thinking not of their feelings but only of what he wanted from them. However, his manipulations didn't work on Rita, no matter how hard he tried. She saw right though his games and stopped him every time. The turning point in the movie and in Phil's life came when he realized that he loved Rita because of a certain character trait she had—her kindness to people—and that he would never win her heart until he became worthy of her. In other words, he realized that he needed to change: he needed to work on product development.

Imagine the following scenario: a man decides he wants to buy a $1,000 stereo system—but he only has $500. So he stops at a flower shop on the way to the music store and buys a bouquet of flowers. He walks into the music store and says to the salesperson, "I'd like to buy that $1,000 stereo, so here is $500 and I bought you some flowers, too." It's crazy! However, this is essentially what some people do when it comes to dating: instead of working on themselves to become worthy of a great person, they try to make up for it with superficialities such as marketing gimmicks and sales maneuvers in order to attain the relationship.

Most likely you are not the cruel animal Phil started out being. But there is probably some aspect of yourself that you can improve. In addition, unlike Phil, you don't have to totally transform yourself to succeed at product development. (Many people do end up transforming themselves over time, but if you start with this goal, you will be overwhelmed and may not begin the product development process at all.)

Before we move on, we'd like to share an insight with you. Often people resist change or improvement because they believe that to concede that something about their character could be improved is the same as saying that something is wrong with them. From a Jewish perspective, this couldn't be further from the truth. Our faults are not our true self. As an analogy, imagine you have a very expensive coat, worth at least $1,000. You go to a party, and someone tells you, "There's a paint spot on your coat." Sure enough, there is a small stain of paint. Would you become angry with the person? Would you respond defensively, "Well, no one's perfect!" Of course you wouldn't, because you recognize that the coat is not you—the stain is no reflection of your worth as a human being. The paint stain is not the coat, and it can be fixed! From a Jewish perspective, we are not our negative qualities. Our flaws were given to us as challenges to try to fix—and that's it. The true essence of every person is pure and good. The rest are just paint spots that need to be cleaned up.

getting practical with product development

A practical advantage to working on product development is that it allows you to move forward with your goal of finding a long-term relationship, even when you are not currently dating. No longer do the intervals between dates need to be unproductive!

So how does product development on yourself work? To

begin with, take a look at yourself—at home, in the grocery store, in traffic(!), at work. Find some aspect of your character that can be improved. Kelly, a SpeedDater, did this exercise and decided she wanted to work on patience—she noticed that she occasionally lost her temper with friends and subordinates at work, and this was not the kind of person she wanted to be.

To begin to work on patience, we told Kelly to find small—actually, tiny—areas in her life where she could practice demonstrating more patience. It's important to start small. Trying to change too much too soon is typically overwhelming and leads to frustration and quitting the process. Kelly decided that on her way to work she would not get angry in traffic. She would give all drivers the benefit of the doubt—even the ones who cut her off! In addition, she would be very careful in grocery stores not to lose her temper in the checkout line with slower-than-average cashiers.

Again, notice that Kelly set herself up for success by making very small changes—only on her drive to work would she commit to being patient in traffic, and only at the grocery (not in the drugstore or other stores) would she practice patience while waiting in line. Kelly is building her patience muscles. By accumulating small wins, Kelly will stay positive about the process because she sees that she can change.

After approximately four months, Kelly expanded her efforts to include all situations in traffic and all types of stores. By slowly building her patience muscle in these small ways, Kelly naturally became more patient with friends and subordinates at work.

SpeedDating Exercise

1. List five aspects of your character you'd like to improve.

2. Choose one (and only one!) to focus on for now.

3. Envision how you would like to be (versus how you are now).

4. Find a few small ways to change this aspect of your life now. Make sure they are 100 percent doable!

5. When you are successful at changing in small ways, reward yourself with something you would not usually buy or do.

6. Now, move the bar a bit higher: find other ways to improve yourself.

Be patient with yourself! It may take a year or more to change one aspect of your character. Give yourself small, achievable goals along the way and enjoy the process!

what do i like and respect about myself?

In the Bible, we learn the famous saying, "Love your neighbor like yourself." Typically the translation focuses upon the loving-of-the-neighbor part. However, of primary importance is to love and respect ourselves! And the extent to which we can love ourselves is the absolute extent to which we can truly love another. Unfortunately, the ability to love oneself is extremely difficult for many people. We would go so far as to say that low self-esteem, or low self-image, is the default position of many people we meet today.

We find that low self-esteem is a root cause of many singles' inability to find or develop a lifelong relationship. Even if you're confident that you have a strong, healthy self-image, it is important to be able to recognize signs of low self-esteem in others so you can understand the ramifications of being in a relationship with someone who has low self-esteem.

A person with low self-esteem, as defined by psychiatrist Dr. Avraham Twerski, consciously or unconsciously believes herself to be much less capable and likeable than she actually is. Low self-esteem can affect anyone, even people who are remarkably successful. In fact, often those we think would be the least susceptible to low self-esteem suffer from it the most. Never assume a brilliant résumé guarantees healthy self-esteem.

In this section we'll explain the importance of healthy self-esteem as it relates to relationships and give you a glimpse of some of the ways low-self esteem manifests itself. We'll also look at how low self-esteem directly inhibits finding and maintaining healthy, long-term relationships.

the most important relationship in your life

While you seek a meaningful and enduring relationship with another person, it is important to realize that you have a more primary relationship—your relationship with yourself. How someone treats himself is one of the biggest clues to how that person will handle a relationship with someone else.

Being good at relationships is a character trait—and character traits are generally consistent across circumstances. The extent to which you can build a good relationship with yourself is directly related to the extent to which you will be able to build a solid relationship with someone else. For example, if someone has an abusive relationship with himself—berating himself for making mistakes or pushing himself beyond healthy limits—this tendency will emerge with others close to him. As such, your relationship with yourself directly affects your relationship with others.

The good news is that with effort, a character trait can be improved. If you work on your relationship with yourself, you'll improve your chances of finding and building a strong relationship with someone else.

healthy
self-esteem

In the Talmud, it is said that a man by the name of Hillel declared, "If I am here, everything is here. If I am not here, woe to the world."

What type of person would make such an arrogant statement? In truth, Hillel is known in Jewish tradition as one of the most humble men who ever lived. How could a man of humility say such a thing? The answer can be found in the definition of self-esteem. From a Jewish perspective, self-esteem comes from understanding two things. The first is that we each have a unique role to play in history. Just as no two people look exactly alike, neither do any two people share the same role. Each person is put on Earth to fulfill her own unique mission. No one else can fulfill another's role. Understanding that we have an important and unique role in this world that no one else can replicate or replace is the first component of self-esteem.

Now consider this: Hillel was a woodchopper. He was desperately poor, eking out a living for his wife and children by cutting wood. Still, central to his emotional reality was his understanding that his role in the universe was unique and important—even though to an outsider he may have appeared as "just a woodchopper."

The second component of self-esteem is trusting that we have everything we need to fulfill this role, and that if we don't have it, we have access to it. Hillel was confident that since he was put here on Earth with this important and unique role, God had given him the tools he needed to accomplish his mission.

So when Hillel said, "If I am here, everything is here," he meant that he knows he was put in the world to accomplish a mission and that he has everything he needs to fulfill it. When Hillel says, "If I am not here, woe to the world," he is recognizing that when he leaves the world, his departure will leave a void. And this is true for *all* of us. Jewish tradition states that when a person dies, it's as if an entire world has died.

Hillel rose from his woodchopping career to become one of the greatest Jewish scholars in history. His healthy self-esteem enabled him to accomplish acts of greatness because he carried the empowering idea that he could accomplish anything he put his mind to and that God was on his side, helping him to achieve his destined role.

We encourage you to consider that you have a special role to play that makes you unique and that you have all the tools you need to accomplish your mission—or access to them.

We've noticed that it is not unusual for people to mistakenly believe that the exact traits or characteristics that make them unique are what is wrong with them. Lisa came to see us because she believed that men just didn't like her. Lisa had been dating for years, but none of the relationships had lasted longer than a couple of months. She was bright, outgoing, direct, and open. One of her core values was honesty. In line with this value, she was always very open with the men she dated. She found that this scared them off.

As she told us her story, she began to cry, saying that she believed that there was something wrong with her; that she needed to become more reserved. As we got to know Lisa, we could tell there was nothing wrong with her. While we all have areas in our lives that we could improve, this is normal and doesn't mean there is something wrong with us. In Lisa's case, what she believed was "abnormal" about her was actually a core characteristic of her uniqueness: her ability to be open and honest with others. This is a characteristic to be nurtured, not suppressed!

As we worked with Lisa, it became clear to her that the only modification necessary was the pace at which she dated. She had a mistaken belief that because she wanted to be an honest person, she had to reveal her deepest ideals and thoughts to her dates very early in the process of dating—usually by the first or second date. Often, within a week or two of meeting someone, she would tell him all about herself and how she felt about him and the potential of a relationship. By simply slowing down the rate at which she revealed her feelings to others, she was able to give the other person the space he needed to form opinions of and develop feelings for her.

how to tell
if someone
has healthy
self-esteem

People with strong self-esteem take care of themselves physically and emotionally. They are aware of their needs and make sure those needs are met, while respecting the needs of others and often helping others meet their own needs. Translated into daily life, self-care means such things as getting sufficient sleep, eating healthfully, and getting moderate amounts of exercise. All these actions are rooted in a feeling of self-worth. This is diametrically opposed to people with low self-esteem who take care of themselves physically to compensate for a deeply felt inferiority to others or fear of rejection.

From an emotional perspective, healthy self-esteem enables people to risk letting others get to know them, even if there may be a risk of rejection. In addition, people with healthy self-esteem are strong enough to leave a doomed relationship because they know that it is not in their best interest in the long term. They have confidence that a better relationship awaits them.

Another characteristic of self-esteem is humility. Often, humility is incorrectly defined as the denial of one's accomplishments. The Jewish tradition defines a humble person as one who is very aware of his accomplishments but who does not boast about them because he recognizes that his talents are gifts from God. When Hillel became a great scholar, he did not brag about it because he realized that he had been given the gift of intelligence and the energy to actualize that potential. Secondly, he recognized that because he had been given these talents, it was his obligation to use them to the best of his ability.

People with healthy self-esteem don't need to brag, because they feel an inner confidence in their accomplishments. How others view them is not very important. To someone with low self-esteem, the opinion of others is paramount.

how low self-esteem can manifest itself on a date

You may find that a person with low self-esteem is unable to work on himself. In other words, the "product development" we spoke about in Question 7 has been scaled back or even shut down. This person's ego is so fragile that if he or someone else sheds light on something about him that is not perfect, he can't handle it. He tends to hear even mild criticism as "You're a bad person."

Judy and Jeremy were on their second date. During dinner Jeremy was excitedly telling a story when, unbeknownst to him, a small piece of food flew out of his mouth and landed on Judy's plate. A look of disgust flashed across Judy's face. Noticing it, Jeremy stopped mid-sentence and asked, "What? What?" "Oh, nothing," Judy said, not wanting to embarrass Jeremy. Jeremy persisted, demanding to know why she had flinched. "Well," Judy replied, "while you were talking, you spit food at me, and that's kind of gross."

How did Jeremy respond? How would you have responded? Jeremy exploded and started to insult Judy. "Well, I wouldn't expect to have my table manners criticized by someone who dumps her drink all over the place," he snapped, referring to Judy's spilling her drink earlier that evening. Judy apologized, saying, "I'm sorry. I didn't mean to hurt your feelings, but . . ." Nonetheless, the date was ruined. Jeremy sulked for the rest of the evening and sent her a terse e-mail the next day.

How would a person with healthy self-esteem have handled the situation? He would simply have apologized to Judy for the social faux pas and continued with his story. He might even have made a gentle, self-deprecating joke about it. It's a sign of healthy self-esteem when a person can laugh at himself.

A date's low self-esteem can also manifest itself in constant talking or bragging about himself. Such people ironically are often labeled as arrogant, when in fact they're simply struggling to communicate to others that they are worthwhile human beings.

SpeedDating Exercise

Below is a self-assessment on your relationship with yourself:

1. Notice how you respond to criticism. Do you get defensive? Or are you able to evaluate the criticism with minimal emotion?

2. Notice your internal "tapes" or self-talk. Do they criticize you or support you? If you are constantly criticizing yourself, try to change the tapes in your head to 80 percent positive self-talk, and only 20 percent criticism. If you never criticize yourself, begin to think of ways you can improve.

3. Make a list of all your positive qualities.

4. Take a list of your negative qualities. Keep in mind that everyone is imperfect, so don't be discouraged by this list. Learn to accept yourself as you are, keeping in mind that you will be working on yourself over time as discussed in Question 7.

who is my team?

 Just as a coach helps an athlete maximize her potential, so a well-selected group of people can help a SpeedDater find a good relationship. Your team will help you maintain objectivity while dating, act as role models, and be anchors in times of challenge, including rejection.

It's unrealistic to expect that one person can handle all these responsibilities. For example, your role model may not have time to help you stay objective while you're dating.

Had it not been for the objective perspective of our teams, we might not be married today. As we mentioned in Question 2, while Sue admired many qualities in Yaacov's character, she doubted his ability to function in the "real" world outside the yeshiva. A year after the car accident incident, we were both in

Israel at the same time. Coincidentally a couple Sue met on her first weekend in Israel recommended that she meet Yaacov! Sue would probably have said no, but her date coach spoke highly of Yaacov and had often tried to persuade Sue to reconsider. Now, with another couple recommending Yaacov, plus her coach's advice, Sue decided to try again. Sure enough, a few hours of serious dating conversation enabled Sue to realize that there was more to Yaacov than she had initially seen.

the dynamics of the dating team in more detail

Keeping Your Objectivity

As we've mentioned, emotions often outpace intellect when dating. It is virtually impossible to stay objective when face-to-face with an attractive date. When emotions take control, you'll possibly distort facts and create an illusion of who you are dating, putting you at risk of falling into Shaping, Avoiding, Selfish, Shooting Star, or other destructive relationships (see Questions 1, 2, and 6).

Remember Eric from Question 2, who was dating Beth, the former Olympic gymnast? About a month after Eric started dating Beth, she accepted an invitation to brunch with her ex-boyfriend. She did not tell Eric—he found out from someone who saw them. Even though he and Beth had agreed to date exclusively, Eric brushed off the fact that Beth hadn't told him about the date. He "loved" Beth and couldn't consider even the *possibility* that she had lapses in commitment, openness, and honesty.

Had Eric been SpeedDating, he would have discussed this incident with a team member to get an objective perspective. We would have told him to slow down the relationship and stay alert and objective.

Team Member #1: Your Date Coach

A date coach is someone whose judgment about relationships you admire, someone you can trust with the details of your SpeedDating process, and someone who has the time to help you evaluate your dating experiences. This person may be a professional counselor or therapist, or simply someone who is open to facilitating your SpeedDating process, such as a friend or relative. You need to feel comfortable telling your date coach how you really feel, even if you suspect you are thinking or acting illogically.

Alison began dating Steve because she was very attracted to him. Steve was kind, athletic, and intelligent. As a Speed-Dater, Alison had become aware of her attraction to irresponsible men. She relied on Sue and a professional counselor to help her see Steve objectively. The following conversation occurred countless times between Alison and Sue: "He's so nice to me, and he really wants to finish college," Alison would say. Sue would respond, "Okay, let's look at the facts as you have told them to me. Steve is twenty-nine years old, he dropped out of college at twenty, he has never held a job for longer than six months, and his car is filled with trash and dirty clothes. Can you tell me anything about Steve's actions that would indicate that he is responsible or beginning to develop a sense of responsibility?" Alison knew intellectually that Sue was right, but she needed this reality check repeatedly. Dating Steve was emotionally confusing for Alison, because she respected many of his core character traits, such as his kindness and sensitivity. In addition, he was gorgeous. Alison's emotions wanted the relationship to work, and these emotions tried hard to shield her intellect from seeing the problems. By leaning on Sue and her sessions with her therapist, Alison had the strength to break up with Steve, and not go back to him even when he continued to pursue her.

Team Member #2: Your Role Models

If a picture is worth a thousand words, so too is watching and learning from someone who has what you want—a lasting relationship. If you did not grow up in a home that fostered healthy relationships, seek out people who have achieved them.

In Question 4, we met Nina. Nina had grown up in a dysfunctional home. She had no clear idea how a healthy relationship functioned. As part of incorporating the principles of SpeedDating into her life, she sought out a family she admired and spent time with them. She joined them for many dinners and volunteered to help with the children on family outings. She grew to understand the dynamics of a healthy relationship and began to incorporate them into her life.

It may be helpful to have several role models. You may admire one friend's approach to dating, the way another handles marital disagreements, and how yet another couple manages their finances. A composite of different aspects of many couples may help you to envision the type of relationship you are seeking and recognize it when it's within reach.

Team Member #3: Your Anchors

Even SpeedDaters will face rejection. And rejection—whether you're the rejecter or the rejected—can be painful, even when you know that ending the relationship is the right decision. In such times you need anchors—people and activities that remind you that you don't need an unhealthy relationship to feel good and enjoy life.

Some of your anchors may not even know that they're part of your SpeedDating team. You may have an acquaintance with whom you enjoy skiing, or watching movies. This person may not be a confidant, but always buoys your spirits.

Anchors can also be hobbies or anything that gives you joy and perhaps adds to your self-esteem and confidence.

An Unseen Team Member

According to Jewish tradition, you can help bring a blessing into your life, including finding your soul mate, by verbally expressing your desire for it to God. The belief is that the universe is full of potential blessing, and by articulating what you want and why you want it, you can pull this blessing into reality. The tradition states that sometimes a person is destined for good, but that good can only come down by privately vocalizing a desire for it. Traditionally, this expression is done through the medium of prayer. If you believe in God, tell God what you want and why you want it. If you don't believe in God, consider expressing your wish anyway—there's no downside; it's personal and private. There is something remarkably powerful about putting your desires into the universe and allowing the universe to help you find what you are looking for.

Keeping Your Dating Experiences within Your Team

Sometimes people feel obligated or compelled to tell others about their budding relationships. But there is a saying in Judaism: "Blessing comes to that which is hidden." In other words, the less you share your business, the more likely your endeavor will be successful.

By limiting your discussions about your dating experiences to your team, you are ensuring that only those you trust will know details about your life. In addition, select team members who will not gossip about you or your experiences.

SpeedDating Exercise

Assemble your team:

1. Find a date coach.

2. Seek out role models and spend time with them on a regular basis.

3. Think about what "anchors" you have—make a list of people you can call and activities you can do when you need support.

do i trust this is going to work out— that i will find my soul mate?

There is a final step to preparing to SpeedDate. It involves asking yourself whether you truly believe that you can find a meaningful, lasting relationship, and then developing a way to maintain that belief if you have it, or build it if you do not.

When people have a general confidence that life can and often does work out for the best, they exude a certain type of happiness. In Hebrew it's called *simcha*. This is not an unrealistic happiness that assumes that life and dating will be easy. Life is a series of challenges. A person with *simcha* faces life's challenges with optimism that the challenge can be resolved, or if it cannot, that some good can be found in it or may come from it.

This internal confidence that things do work out for the good is important for three reasons.

1. Happiness and Trust Are Attractive

A happy person, a person filled with *simcha,* exudes a special attractiveness. We're sure you've met people who have a certain positive energy, or charisma, that attracts people to them. It is not uncommon for these people to appear quite average in appearance or talents—yet they exude an internal beauty and animation that makes people want to be around them.

Think of working on becoming more trusting and more filled with *simcha* as both product development and marketing rolled into one (see Question 7). Becoming happier will improve your character as well as your attractiveness.

We used to have a neighbor named Linda who was exceptionally beautiful, but extremely cynical about her chances of finding a man who would appreciate her. She had had many bad experiences with men and had come to believe that men were basically not to be trusted. So great were her cynicism, bitterness, and lack of trust that it showed in her face. In addition, she typically made snap judgments about her dates. The smallest of actions, like her date not opening the door for her, would be interpreted as a sign of a character flaw. At a deep level, Linda did not believe she would find her partner—and this fear became a reality.

People like Linda date in ways that are not effective and then begin to believe that dating doesn't work or that good people don't exist. As we've discussed, the problem is not with other people so much as it is with the traditional dating process. The process of SpeedDating enables people to have positive dating experiences and to regain their trust in the dating process.

2. Happiness and Trust Build Confidence

Trust and a general sense of happiness give you the confidence you need to walk away from relationships that are not working. People sometimes stay in unhealthy relationships because they don't believe they will find anyone else. In Question 1 we met Jane, who was holding onto her relationship with John, the sports car racing enthusiast. Jane kept insisting that she would never meet anyone as wonderful as John—even though she was trying to change one of his core values! In other words, she doubted that she would ever find what she was looking for— someone who had John's character traits but a different direction in life.

Jane became a SpeedDating volunteer and helped organize events and seminars. Over time she realized the mistake she was making and was able to build enough trust to leave her relationship with John. Today she is open to meeting new people and truly believes she will find a meaningful relationship.

3. Happiness and Trust Open You to Finding Your Soul Mate

The third reason for developing trust has a spiritual dimension. From a spiritual perspective, *simcha* plays a powerful role in helping people find their soul mate. In the Jewish tradition it is held that just as there are physical laws like gravity and the speed of light, so there are spiritual laws. One of these spiritual laws is that the trust that good things will and do happen conducts blessing into the world. In other words, happy people are more likely to have good things happen to them—or more precisely, they are more likely to create good situations and overcome difficult challenges.

From a secular (nonspiritual) perspective, this dynamic has been described as "the power of positive thinking." There is a deep spiritual truth embedded in this popular self-help concept. It may be the most important reason why it is important to focus on developing a positive attitude.

This concept is the reverse of what is commonly thought. Many people believe that happiness comes from receiving blessing. What we're saying is that a person who has an attitude of happiness attracts blessing.

While Sue was in graduate school, she interviewed many successful businesspeople. The primary similarity she discovered among them was a positive attitude, despite the fact that all of them had at one time or many times experienced personal or business failures, including bankruptcy. Their belief that things could be better and would eventually work out enabled them to maintain their persistence and not lose hope.

It's easy to say that people who have successful relationships are lucky. Not so, we say. Most likely they have worked very hard on their attitude and on their relationship. Their effort to maintain a positive focus enabled them to find the right relationship and maintain it.

how to build and maintain trust

SpeedDating Success Rates

One way to build trust is to look at the success rate among people who have used the principles on which SpeedDating is based. The vast majority of SpeedDaters who are focused on finding a meaningful relationship and who don't lose hope find their soul mate. It sometimes takes a few years—but it usually happens!

In the ten years we have watched singles apply these principles, we have only in a few rare instances seen people not achieve their goal. Our teachers, with over forty years' experience teaching these principles, relate similar success rates.

If someone with the goal of losing weight acts on this goal by eating right and exercising regularly, it's likely that she'll accomplish the goal. There are some people who, for medical or psychological reasons, will not be able to achieve this goal. However, these instances are rare. So it is with SpeedDating: if you truly apply the principles, you will most likely find the relationship you are seeking.

Use Your Team!

It's unrealistic to expect ourselves to build and maintain trust alone. We need friends (or sometimes professional counselors)

to lean on when times are difficult. Dating can be difficult—
even SpeedDating!

The first person Sue date-coached was a twenty-eight-
year-old woman named Cari. She was committed to following
the principles of SpeedDating, yet petrified that she wouldn't
find a meaningful relationship. Cari would call Sue regularly
with the same concern: "There are so many women who have
been dating for years [using the principles behind SpeedDating]
who are still single!" "Who?" Sue would ask. "Lots," Cari
would answer. "There's Jane." "Who has only been applying
SpeedDating principles for two years and is forty-two years
old. It sometimes does take longer for older women—but you
are twenty-eight and have only been SpeedDating for a couple
of months!" "Well, what about Erica?" Cari would ask.

"Erica is in the middle of medical school and isn't sure she
wants to commit to a relationship until after she graduates."
And so the conversation would go.

To build and maintain trust in the process, Cari would call
Sue whenever her fears became overwhelming. She knew her
doubts put her at risk of falling into faux relationships. Without
trusting that SpeedDating would work, she would have held
onto unhealthy relationships for fear she would find no one
else.

During the two years that Sue coached Cari, Cari witnessed many of her "examples of failure" find their soul
mates. At age forty-three Jane found hers, and today is the
mother of a healthy girl. Erica is still in a four-year residency
program. She doesn't perceive herself as a failure in Speed-
Dating—she has made a choice that for now she's going to

focus on her career. And Cari found her special person at the age of thirty.

If trusting that you will find your soul mate is challenging for you, it is especially important to include someone on your team who can help you build that trust—someone who can listen to your doubts and fears regardless of how often they surface. Even if you do have a deep trust that you'll reach your goal, the process can become challenging and doubts can arise. Sometimes you need someone to help pull you out of your fears.

There are times when people call us and say, "Listen, I know this is just a crazy fear, but I need some encouragement." At those times we simply listen to their fears, respond to them, and remind them of the success others have had and of the fallacies of traditional dating.

SpeedDating Exercise

1. Take a minute to ask yourself, Do I trust that this is going to work out? Do I trust that I will find my soul mate?

2. Write down your answer and why you feel this way.

3. Regardless of whether you answered yes, no, or in between, go back to your team list. See if there is anyone on your list in whom you can confide if you begin to doubt yourself. If not, then think about who you can add to the list who will talk you through your doubts and fears.

dating the speeddating way

> ## Essential Questions to Ask Yourself, Your Date, and Your Team while Dating

In Part 1 we focused on preparing to date. In Part 2 we explore the practicalities of how to date—specifically how to decrease the chance of your wasting time in doomed relationships. Typically SpeedDaters can weed out doomed relationships in a handful of dates, rather than in nine months or years. In addition, SpeedDaters can usually tell if a relationship is the right one within about four months.

SpeedDaters learn this so quickly because SpeedDating is really "speed learning" about another person and the potential of a relationship. The purpose of SpeedDating is not entertainment—its pur-

pose is to learn relatively quickly who you are dating and whether the relationship has potential. The speed learning is accomplished by using the techniques we'll discuss in Part 2. Most of these techniques focus on helping the SpeedDater stay objective. When you are face-to-face with an attractive date, it's all too easy to lose objectivity and begin to dub in, so to speak, your fantasy of this person in place of the reality.

In this section we assume that you are dating someone now or are ready to do so. We will examine two types of questions to ask during the dating process. The first type, which we call SpeedDating strategy questions, continue the process you began in Part 1 of exploring essential principles of relationships that apply throughout dating—from first meeting someone to deciding to commit to that person. The other types, which we call SpeedDating pacing questions, are questions to ask on a specific date or at a particular time in the process of dating. We include these questions because we are often asked, "What should we ask on the first date? The second date?" etc. It's difficult to answer these questions generally, but we have provided some loose guidelines as to what questions to ask during the different phases of dating. ★ Don't feel bound to follow this sequence, as people feel comfortable getting to know others at different rates. Some people, however, find that the pace at which they date is interfering with their success in finding a meaningful relationship. Those of you who feel you need a clearer timeline in your dating may find these pacing guidelines helpful.

Let's continue!

---

*For guidelines on how to approach a seven-minute date, see Appendix A. For sample questions to ask on a seven-minute date, see Appendix B.

question 11

do i enjoy being with this person?

The first date! There may be nothing more exciting and more nerve-racking.

From the SpeedDating perspective, the first and second dates should be (theoretically) the easiest of all your dates because there is only one question to ask yourself: Do I enjoy being with this person? You shouldn't expect that anything heavy will happen on these dates—no revealing of innermost thoughts, dreams, and feelings, and certainly, absolutely certainly, no physical intimacy (more about that in Question 14, "Is This Relationship Ready for Physical Intimacy?"). We like to say that the first two dates are not to find out if this is the person of your dreams, but simply to find out if this person is *not* the person of your dreams.

One of the mistakes we see singles make on first dates is

assuming that if they don't have a "wow" feeling—a sense of intense chemistry—on the first date, the relationship has no chance for success. This assumption has probably kept more potentially happy couples apart than most other false beliefs. In Question 2 we discussed the beauty of the Buried Treasure relationship. The hallmark of such a relationship is that the initial feelings are not intense. The attraction grows over time, as the couple gets to know each other.

Here is how to handle your feelings on the first date. (In Question 12 we'll discuss how to handle your thoughts and emotions throughout the entire dating process.) If you don't sense anything truly negative about the person—in fact, if you find yourself saying, "Well, he's a nice guy"—then date him again! Don't be so quick to dismiss someone just because you didn't feel an intense connection on the first meeting.

Debbie was thirty-nine and not married. We had known her for years, and during that time she had gone out on a myriad of first dates, but nothing had blossomed into a relationship. In fact, very few had even gone past the first date. She confided to us that she meets lots of "nice guys," but none that she finds really exciting and dynamic.

Subconsciously Debbie was evaluating each first date on whether or not she felt an immediate chemistry. Essentially, she was asking herself, Do I feel crazy about this guy? When the answer was no, she'd assume the relationship had no future. In truth, it's probably a sign of psychological health not to fall head over heals for someone on the first meeting: healthy people typically don't bare their souls to strangers.

That's why the question to ask is, Do I enjoy being with this person? You may have concerns about the viability of the relationship, but most of those questions can wait until future dates. The idea on the first date is to decide whether you want to see this person again, rather than make snap judgments about the viability of a long-term relationship—another mistake we see many singles make. Many people try to read too much into their date's comments or actions on the first date, when in reality there is no way of knowing what those words or actions really mean at that early stage of dating. (In Question 13 we'll discuss how to evaluate someone's actions and words accurately.)

A key to a successful first date is to ask fun, nonthreatening questions that elicit intriguing (you hope!) information about the other person, such as:

- What are your three favorite movies? Why?
- What is your favorite book? Why?
- What was your first childhood job?
- What do you remember about your kindergarten teacher?
- Did you ever own a pet? What was its name? Why?
- Where is the most beautiful place you visited?
- Are you a "large picture" or "small details" type of person?

These are just a few sample questions—make your own list! But keep in mind that a date is not an interrogation. If the question feels fun to ask, it's probably a good question. As you get to know each other on this date, try to keep an open mind throughout the date and only evaluate it afterward.

A third common mistake we see is the budding Shooting Star relationship we discussed in Question 2. A couple goes out on one or two dates, feels a strong connection, and then rushes into an intimate relationship—both emotionally and physically. As we've discussed previously, if you feel this chemistry on the first couple of dates, take it as a good sign, but don't assume the relationship is destined to last just because you feel this way. Take the time to get to know your date, and then see if the chemistry is still there once you really know who you are dating.

Another mistake we see singles make is to begin dating someone when they are already dating someone else. Dating multiple people at one time is confusing and can often bring heartache. Renee and Brad had been dating for a couple of months. Everything seemed to be going well, when all of a sudden Brad stopped calling Renee. When she finally reached him, Brad told her that he was very busy at work but he would call her when his schedule cleared. Renee could tell this was the end of their dating relationship. Within a few weeks Renee learned that Brad had been dating another woman simultaneously. She learned that while they were dating and Brad was professing how much he cared about her, he had taken a romantic weekend trip with the other woman.

Another complication of dating more than one person simultaneously is that when you are dating person A, you are constantly comparing person A to person B. This distorts your ability to judge clearly. Ideally you should date one person, make a decision about that person, and only after deciding not to commit, accept a date with someone else.

what are my thoughts telling me—which should i listen to, and which should i ignore?

 This question will help you more clearly identify your own biases and therefore be in a better position to evaluate *accurately* your date in the shortest amount of time.

We all have thoughts running through our heads all day long—and, if you include dreams, all night long as well. These thoughts typically come from either our intellect or our emotions and generally can be categorized as constructive or destructive.

Any rational decision is comprised of input from both our intellect and our emotions. However, most people let their emotions dominate their thinking in matters of the heart. For successful SpeedDating you need to listen to both intellect and emotions in order to make the best decision. That's why, as a first step, it is important to be aware of *all* your thoughts.

This awareness is crucial because our thoughts drive our actions. So, if you consciously choose which thoughts to listen to, you will be more in control of your actions.

Let's look at an example:

Sandy, a graduate student, began dating Bill, a successful businessman seven years her senior. Sandy was very spiritual, had a strong belief in a higher power, and wanted to find a man with similar views who would appreciate this aspect of her. Bill had made a decision years ago that he was an agnostic rationalist. Within a few weeks of dating Sandy, he made it known that there was no way anyone would ever convince him of the existence of a higher power. "You just can never know for sure" was his unwavering opinion.

Sandy began learning the principles of SpeedDating after she and Bill had been dating for almost two years. She was unable to decide whether or not to break up with Bill. To help her clarify the situation, she identified her thoughts about the relationship:

- I feel safe when I'm around him.
- I don't respect his views on spirituality.
- I'm disgusted by how much time he spends watching TV.
- I respect that he became a professional/expert in his field and has a successful career.

Then she considered each of those thoughts, exploring whether other thoughts or feelings lay beneath them. She also identified whether each thought was coming from her intellect or her emotions:

- I feel safe when I'm around him (emotion).
  - I'm just starting my own career and have a lot of fears about whether I will be able to support myself financially—so this is probably why I feel safe around Bill. He is financially secure and has a strong professional skill.

- I don't respect his views on spirituality (intellect).
  - I believe strongly in a higher power, but Bill is an adamant agnostic. He says no one and nothing will ever convince him otherwise—he believes you can never know for sure.
  - As I think about this, I realize this is a deal breaker for me. I want to be with someone who shares a similar spiritual view to my own because spirituality is such a large part of my life, I want to be able to share it with someone else and with our children.

- I'm disgusted by how much time he spends watching TV (emotion).
  - My opinion is that watching TV is a waste of time for the most part. Bill often spends all day Sunday in front of the TV.
  - I guess this is a value that I hold and Bill has a different value—for him watching TV is a way to unwind, relax, and prepare for the week.

- I respect that he is a professional/expert in an area and has a successful career (intellect).
  - Since I am just beginning my career and have a lot of fears about my chances for success, I respect anyone who has worked hard and developed an area of expertise. However, I see that this isn't a basis for a relationship.

Sandy reviewed this list with us. We asked her, "If you were already successful at your career and did not have to worry about finances, would you still be dating Bill?" Sandy's answer was, "Probably not."

By systematically analyzing her thoughts, Sandy was able to recognize that she and Bill should break up. She saw that she was using him by holding on to the relationship, especially since he seriously wanted to marry her. Moreover, by prolonging the relationship, Sandy was preventing herself from meeting her soul mate and keeping Bill from doing the same.

combating irrational thoughts

Now came the hard part: Sandy needed to break up with Bill. They had been dating for almost two years because Sandy had been listening to her emotions—her fears of financial and professional failure—and minimizing input from her intellect.

Even though Sandy now knew that she and Bill needed to break up, she just couldn't muster the strength to end the relationship. We helped Sandy explore this by continuing the exercise of examining her thoughts. She discovered that one thought kept nagging at her: "I'll never be able to support myself financially. I'm going to end up a bag lady."

Everyone has destructive, irrational thoughts—so the question becomes, How do I handle destructive thoughts? The answer is to ignore them.

The first step is to intellectually prove them wrong (if possible). In Sandy's case, she reminded herself that she had graduated from college with good grades, had supported herself financially for over four years, and was now succeeding in graduate school.

For a while, when Sandy had that destructive thought, she would mentally repeat why it was inaccurate. Later she would simply say to herself, "Go away, you're not true—this is simply coming from fear."

Sandy also called on her team. She told one member of her team that this was her current struggle and that if the thought became too strong, she would call this team member and ask her to walk her through the reasoning that would help her banish the thought.

It took Sandy about four months to break up with Bill, but she did it. Had she not been involved with SpeedDating principles, it might have taken her another two years.

when the intellect dominates the emotions

Most people, like Sandy, allow their emotions to dominate their thinking, especially when they're involved in a relationship. However, there are some people whose intellect dominates their emotions, impeding their progress in love.

Kim knew exactly the type of person she was looking for. She had employed SpeedDating techniques and would evaluate each date against various lists and priorities she had developed.

When she began dating Keith, she knew he was perfect! He matched everything on her list. Keith felt the same way about Kim. But something was preventing Kim from accepting Keith's marriage proposal, and she couldn't figure out what it was.

When Kim wrote down all the thoughts she had about the relationship, listing each area of compatibility, she noticed that every thought was coming from her intellect. She decided to introduce Keith to one of her SpeedDating Team members, an elderly woman Kim had known for years. After the three of them met for lunch one Sunday, Kim called her friend to ask what she thought. Her friend said quite matter-of-factly, "There is no chemistry between you two."

Bells went off in Kim's head. Yes! That was it. She had been so focused on intellectualizing the relationship, she had forgotten to listen to the voices from her emotions that were saying, "He's a great guy, but there's nothing here!"

Kim did break up with Keith, and today she is married to her soul mate.

what creates your thoughts

We've mentioned that thoughts drive actions. But what creates your thoughts? For the most part, your desires do. More importantly, those desires will determine which thoughts you'll listen to and act upon. The problem is that desires do not always motivate people to make the best decisions. For example, Sandy's desire for financial security was driving her to maintain her relationship with Bill and assume that it had long-term potential. Her desire had created false thoughts.

Most people, regardless of their desires, also have thoughts that reflect the truth. The key is to be able to distinguish true thoughts from false ones.

Once Sandy began the SpeedDating process, she was able to bring her unconscious thoughts into conscious awareness and decide if she wanted her life to be dominated by her desire for financial security. She decided that finding the right person was more important than her craving for security, and was able to find the strength to break up with Bill.

By realizing that desires drive thoughts and thoughts drive actions, you are in a better position to more accurately and quickly evaluate the potential for a relationship to last.

SpeedDating Exercise

1. Become aware of the thoughts that run through your mind throughout the day. Note what types of thoughts you typically have:
- Are they positive?
- Are they negative or destructive?
- Are they coming from emotion?
- Are they coming from intellect?

2. Note your destructive thoughts and strategize how to address them. Find ways of pushing them out of your mind. Consider asking one of your SpeedDating team members to help you. For example, you could call your team member and say, "I keep having this destructive thought that I'll never find anyone." And your team member should be ready to help you combat that negative thought.

3. While you're on a date, notice your thoughts in evaluating the date.
- Are the thoughts coming from your emotions: "Wow, he's so cute!"
- Are the thoughts coming from your intellect: "We share similar life goals! And he has four out of the five character traits I am looking for."
- Are the thoughts from your intellect and emotions consistent with each other, or opposing?
- Are the thoughts destructive: "He'll never want to go out with me again because I said that really stupid thing."

Be sure to listen to both your intellect and emotions and then decide which thoughts you are going to listen to. Keep in mind that the vast majority of people need more input from their intellect. When you have destructive thoughts, combat them by telling yourself that they are not true and you won't listen to negativity.

is this an action, or my interpretation of an action?

In the previous Question we began exploring how to evaluate your date apart from your own personal bias so that you can see the real person, not a fantasy. This Question expands your ability to judge your date objectively by distinguishing between what really happens on the date and how you interpret it.

Suppose a man opens the restaurant door for his date, and she enters ahead of him. The date thinks, "Wow, this man is so kind and considerate. He opened the door for me!" Let's analyze this scenario:

What is the action?	The man opening the door for his date.
What is the interpretation?	The man is kind and considerate.

What is the reality?   We don't know.

When someone opens a door for another person, does it always mean that this person is kind? No. It may simply mean that the person knows social etiquette, or that it was convenient to let the other person enter first. In fact, we really don't know what this person's action means. It may or may not relate to being kind.

Imagine that you were given a 5,000-piece puzzle to assemble—without a photo of the completed puzzle. How many pieces of the puzzle would you have to assemble before you knew what it depicted? Probably at least a few hundred, if not thousands, of pieces. You probably would not start seriously guessing what the puzzle depicted until you had enough pieces connected to make an educated guess. So it should be with dating!

As we've noted, dating is a series of educated guesses about another person. You should not be drawing firm conclusions about another person until you see enough of *his* "picture." When you meet someone for the first time, you don't know anything about him. His actions may or may not represent the character traits you would likely assign to them. In fact, the same action by two different people may represent two very different character traits, depending on the intentions behind the actions. Often we can't know intentions on a first, second, or even third date.

A student of ours, Michelle, called us one day in a panic. She said that she was going to have to break up with her new boyfriend, Rick, because she had learned that he kept a gun in his apartment. To Michelle, keeping a gun in the house was an absolute deal breaker. She assumed that Rick's owning a gun indicated that his character was shifty. Here is Michelle's action/interpretation scenario:

Action:	Rick keeps a gun in his apartment.
Interpretation:	Rick is a shifty character.
Reality:	We don't know what owning a gun indicates about Rick's character.

We suggested to Michelle that two different people could have entirely different reasons for owning a gun. The key would be for Michelle to determine Rick's reason for owning one.

Michelle decided to ask Rick about the gun. He explained that he owned a gun because it was what his family had always done—it seemed normal to him. He was open to not having a gun in the house.

Michelle's initial evaluation of Rick was inaccurate. She had judged Rick before she had enough pieces of the puzzle to understand the full picture. Jumping to conclusions—or, more accurately, "jumping to evaluations"—leads to ineffective dating.

putting the puzzle together: evaluating your date's actions

So, how do we accurately evaluate another person? How do we put the puzzle together? Remember from Question 12 that thoughts drive actions and desires drive thoughts. It is those thoughts and desires that you'll want to understand about your date.

1. The first step is simply to be aware of your date's actions. Note we did not say to notice what you think your date is doing—we're emphasizing that you strive to see your date's "pure action." Also, don't let words take the place of actions. A person can say anything, but if their actions do not reflect their words, then the words are meaningless.

2. Do not prematurely interpret what your date's actions mean. As a rule of thumb on the first couple of dates, note your date's actions but don't be quick to assign an interpretation. Wait until you have enough puzzle pieces before you begin judging the other person.

3. When you have accumulated a bank of actions/puzzle pieces, begin assigning interpretations.

Let's look at a sample SpeedDating first date:

Situation: SpeedDater Jill notices that Dan is twenty minutes late to pick her up.

The action/puzzle piece: Dan arrives twenty minutes after Jill believes they had arranged to meet. (Note that the pure action is not "Dan is late"—that's already an evaluation. It's possible that they miscommunicated about the time of the date.)

Jill's evaluation: Dan is late, or I misunderstood the time we were going to meet. However, I'm positive I heard him correctly. Anyway, if he is late, I don't know him well enough to know if this action is reflective of his character (i.e., being inconsiderate). There may be extenuating circumstance, such as heavy traffic.

Jill's conclusion: I'm going to take note of this action. If he's late in the future, I'll take the action more seriously. In this case, I'll give him the benefit of the doubt and assume that he had an emergency or that we miscommunicated. I will act very understanding when he arrives.

Note that Jill isn't ignoring the action, but she is refraining, for now, from assuming that it signifies something specific about Dan. Dan's arrival time on the first date is simply a puzzle piece. Let's continue.

The action/puzzle piece: Dan arrives and doesn't mention that he is late.

Jill's evaluation: Dan didn't apologize for being late—this is a bit disconcerting.

Jill's conclusion: I'll still give Dan the benefit of the doubt, since this is our first date. Perhaps I heard the time wrong, and he's actually ten minutes early!

Jill is not dismissing Dan's actions, nor is she being naive; she is temporarily suspending judgment. She's extremely aware of Dan's actions, but is careful to distinguish between his actions and her interpretations of them.

more puzzle pieces: words versus actions

Words are not actions. If someone says, "I am very punctual and I try always to be on time," but she is late 90 percent of the time, she is not punctual! She may *want* to be punctual, but she is not.

A key to the SpeedDating process is not to confuse words

with actions. It's important to listen to what a person says, but their words need to be reinforced with actions.

Anna had been dating Richard for three weeks when Richard told her he loved her. Anna, being a SpeedDater, asked Richard what he loved about her. Richard was able to list a number of her qualities that he admired. However, Anna did not immediately assume that he truly loved *her*. She looked for more pieces of the puzzle—actions he had done—that would demonstrate his love. Given that they had only gone on four dates, she could not find an example of his showing concern and care for her in a deep and thoughtful way. This doesn't mean that Richard didn't love her; realistically, four dates may not provide the opportunity to demonstrate deep caring and concern. Here's what the action/interpretation scenario looked like:

Action:	On the fourth date Richard tells Anna he loves her.
Anna's interpretation:	Maybe Richard loves me, maybe he doesn't—so far, no significant action indicates his love or concern for me.
Reality:	We don't know at this time.

Laurie came to talk to us about problems she was having in her marriage. Her husband, Sam, had been in and out of work for the four years since their wedding. We asked Laurie if he had demonstrated this job instability when they were dating. At first Laurie shook her head—"No, not at all." Then she paused and said, "Well, in the two years we dated he had four jobs—but he always had a good reason for leaving each job."

Had Laurie been following the SpeedDating process, she would have been more attuned to Sam's actions and may have recognized Sam's pattern of job instability, rather than relying solely on his explanations for leaving each job. She still may have decided to marry him, but she would have done so fully aware of the employment challenges she might face in their long-term relationship.

To summarize, when you are dating, be sure to distinguish among the following:

1. Your date's action.
2. The interpretation you give that action.
3. Your date's words.
4. The consistency or inconsistency between your date's words and actions.

SpeedDating Exercise

1. After a date, review the actions, conversations, and interpretations that occurred.

2. If you have been dating for more than three dates, begin to notice patterns, inconsistencies, and consistencies.

3. Discuss your findings with a member of your SpeedDating team to be sure that you're being objective about your date's actions.

is this relationship ready for physical intimacy?

Am I willing to give a part of my soul to this person and carry a part of theirs?

 In the previous three Questions we've focused on learning how to maintain objectivity when dating. There's one sure way to lose this objectivity.

It's probably not what you want to hear, but we'll tell it to you straight: a sure way to lose objectivity about your date is to become physically intimate with your partner before making a commitment★ to the relationship. In other words, all that we've been discussing—getting to know a person's character, where he is heading in life, and his priorities—should be explored, and a lifelong commitment to the relationship should be made, *before* beginning an intimate physical relationship.

When a couple has mutual respect for each other's charac-

★With the current divorce rate approximating 50 percent, some people are cynical about the level of commitment marriage brings. But we and Jewish tradition hold that a lifelong commitment is best expressed through marriage.

ter and life goals and share common values and life direction, they have the basis for forming true intimacy that is rooted in reality. Such a grounded relationship has the potential to continue growing over time. For this couple, physical intimacy is a reflection of the emotional intimacy they've created.

It's tempting to say that we can become physically intimate with someone without the relationship having to be "heavy." But there is something very different between having simply gone to the movies with someone and being physically intimate. Virtually everyone recognizes this difference, and Jewish mysticism has an answer for where this difference comes from.

From a Jewish perspective, physical intimacy is the merging of two souls. This means that when a couple is intimate, their souls actually join, and a part of each soul is exchanged. Thus, when physical intimacy occurs, a spiritual bond is created, whether or not true intimacy exists in the relationship. This is the root of the difference between physical relations and other activities like going to the movies or playing tennis together: physical intimacy creates a bond between the two people. In addition, physical intimacy can cause a lot of confusion, which typically affects men and women differently. Let us explain.

Women feel the bond created by sexual relations and often confuse it with a real emotional bond. This feeling of connection can tie a woman to the wrong man, making her unable to view the relationship objectively. This leads many women into staying in poor or even abusive relationships, because they mistakenly believe that the connection they feel means that the relationship is meant to last. Physical relations can also bind a couple together in avoidance of the terrible feeling of loss that occurs when the relationship ends. People often stay in less-than-optimal relationships because they want to avoid the pain of separation.

Unlike women, men are not usually as sensitive to the bond that develops from physical relations. As such, they will not be as susceptible to clinging to an unsuccessful relationship simply because physical intimacy is involved. In fact, what often happens is that men come to despise the women with whom they have had casual relations, or at least become less attracted to and respectful of them. On a subconscious level, men want a real spiritual connection with another human. They want a meaningful relationship—that's what we all crave. They want to find someone who connects with their eternal self—not just their body, but their soul. When physical relations precede true intimacy, the relationship becomes focused on the physical, noneternal aspect of both partners, leaving less room for true intimacy to develop.

Bottom line: subconsciously men associate women with whom they have casual relations with the aspect of themselves that is mortal. No one wants to see themselves as simply mortal. Most people sense that deep down there is a spiritual, eternal essence to them as well. Casual physical relationships put the mortal ahead of the spiritual, with the ironic result that men will be more likely to lose interest in a relationship the sooner physical intimacy is initiated.

Women, therefore, have good reason for delaying physical intimacy. One reason is to maintain their own objectivity. Another is to avoid the unnecessary heartache that comes from breaking off a sexual relationship. A third is to increase the chances that the man she is dating will continue to be interested in the relationship.

Often when we teach this idea, women respond that if they don't become physically involved with a man within the first three dates, he will break it off. We've found, however, that men who are serious about finding a lifelong, committed relationship are actually relieved to postpone physical intimacy until a true emotional bond has formed. They, too, want to be discriminating about the person to whom they reveal their deepest self. By waiting to have a physically intimate relationship, women will weed out the men who are looking only for a superficial relationship.

Kara, a new SpeedDater, decided not to have relations with a man until they had a committed relationship in the form of marriage. The next man she dated, Devin, took her out to an expensive restaurant on the first date and called her the next day, eager to set up a second date.

On their second date he took her to another beautiful restaurant. During this date Devin made several physical advances, making it clear that he wanted to move their physical relationship forward. On the third date, when Devin's physical advances became even more overt, Kara told him about her new philosophy of physical intimacy. Devin never called Kara again. Kara was stunned. The devoted Devin had been dating her not to get to know her and possibly form a long-term relationship, but solely to have sex. "At first I felt rejected," Kara told us, "but then I felt so relieved that I learned this about Devin after just a few dates. And just think," she said disgustedly, "if I had had relations with him, I would have felt so used!"

A few weeks after her experience with Devin, Kara met Jim, the man who would become her husband. Had she been in a relationship with Devin at the time, she may not have met Jim, or might not have noticed him if she had. This is a primary benefit of SpeedDating: by avoiding relationships with the wrong person, you remain open to finding the right person.

Earlier, we mentioned another reason to delay physical intimacy—to avoid accumulating emotional scars. It's surprising to us how many people are unaware of the emotional damage they can do to themselves and others through casual physical relationships. A teacher of Yaacov's, Rabbi Nachum Braverman, once posed the following scenario to his students: suppose you met a very attractive person in a bar, and there was an immediate and powerful connection between the two of you. If this person suggested that you go back to his/her apartment, would you do it? All the men said yes, and so did some of the women. Now, suppose this same person asked instead to borrow your brand-new $35,000 sports car for the weekend. Would you say yes? The majority of the people in the room said, "No way!" This was an intriguing result: the students were more willing to consider physical intimacy with a stranger than to lend that stranger a new car. Yaacov's teacher asked the class, "Why would you jump into a physical relationship with someone before lending that stranger your car?" "Because the car could get hurt!" the class answered. Implying, of course, that they could not!

We are all aware of physical dangers, yet emotional ones are less apparent to us. It's typically much more painful to leave a relationship that has become physically intimate than a relationship that has not. As we've explained, this pain comes from the bond that intimate relations create. Even a couple that had casual relations has formed a type of spiritual bond that will cause pain when it is broken. In her book *The Magic Touch,* Gila Manolson describes many scenarios in which singles experienced long-term emotional scars from having physical relations outside of marriage. For women, these scars often translate into bitterness; for men they translate into a dulled sensitivity to meaningful relationships.

Our students tend to agree with these views in principle, but reality may be a different matter! It's not easy to remember these ideas in the heat of powerful attraction. Here are some of the objections our students raise.

"this sounds good, but . . ."

Two of the main objections we hear when we talk about delaying an intimate physical relationship are that it just "feels too good not to do it" and it "feels right at the time." However, as we all know, something that "feels good" does not always mean that it *is* good. Chocolate tastes good, but it's not nutritionally good for us.

There is more than one definition for the word *good*. Singles sometimes lose track of the type of "good" they are feeling and confuse a sensual good for a lasting good. Physical intimacy before emotional intimacy and commitment may feel good and right in the moment, but it's not likely to bring lasting, good results. So when you think to yourself, This feels good, reframe the issue and ask yourself, Does this relationship seem like one that's going to last? If you don't yet know the person well and no commitment has been made, the answer is a definite, I don't know, and probably not!

As an aside, Judaism has nothing against physical intimacy. In fact it is viewed as a beautiful and vital part of a healthy, loving, *committed* relationship.

the test drive

Another objection we frequently hear to delaying physical relations is: "We need to know if we're sexually compatible!"

Yes, physical compatibility is very important to a relationship. However, relations before commitment are not going to establish whether you are suited for each other. People are not cars! For one thing, a person's emotional attachment to his car is not going to affect the quality of the car's driving. It will perform the same way whether it is being driven by its owner or by the friend's neighbor who is borrowing it for the weekend.

But with people, emotional involvement and commitment to the relationship will greatly affect the nature and quality of a physical relationship. In fact, some people feel inhibited when having relations with a stranger or with anyone with whom there is no commitment. As such, casual relations may not be satisfying. However, if the couple had waited until an emotional bond had formed and a commitment had been made, they might have had a totally positive and beautiful experience. Even if physical relations are great early on in a relationship, it may fool the couple into thinking a relationship is meant to last before they really know whether they admire each other's character and life goals.

Because it can be difficult to postpone physical intimacy—especially when you feel that tremendous connection with another human being—we recommend that you strategize before the date about how you plan to refrain from relations before a lifelong commitment has been made.

SpeedDating Exercise

Before you begin a physically intimate relationship, ask yourself these questions. If you can't answer these questions, including a "yes" to (**5**), then the relationship is definitely not ready for physical intimacy.

1. What are this person's core character traits?

2. Are these the traits I am looking for in another person?

3. What is this person's life direction?

4. Am I headed in the same direction as this person, or do we at least have a mutual respect for the direction our lives would be going?

5. Have we made a lifelong commitment to the relationship?

question 15

what am i going to learn during *this* date?

Every SpeedDating date has a purpose—to learn a little more about the person you are dating and reveal a little bit more about yourself.

Plan each date, not just where you're going to have dinner or what movie you're going to see, but also what puzzle pieces you want revealed—what information you want to gather on that date. This information does not have to be monumental. It may simply be learning about her family, or about why he chose his career.

Be sure each date includes significant time conducive to talking—at least a half hour, if not longer.

learning about another person

During the first month of dating, you should be collecting puzzle pieces about your date, such as:

- Her character traits
- Her interests
- Her goals
- Where she's headed in life. Does she know?

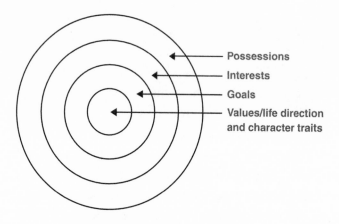

You can start with possessions and interests. These are generally very nonthreatening topics to talk about. You can ask questions such as:

- How do you like to spend your free time?
- What hobbies do you have?

- How did you get involved in that hobby?
- How did you decide to buy a _____ (type of car)?
- How do you like living in (town or city)?
- How did you choose your career?
- What do you find most interesting about your job?
- What do you find most boring about your job?

From these questions about possessions and interests, you probably will begin to glimpse your date's goals, values, and character traits.

As you get to know your date, ask questions that directly aim at learning about goals, values, and character traits. You may feel comfortable asking these questions around Date 3 or 4, or maybe in the second month. Some examples include:

- What is your greatest accomplishment?
- Where do you see yourself in five years, and how do you see yourself getting there?
- How do you see yourself prioritizing family and career?
- Do you want to have children? Why or why not?
- What do you want most for your children? How are you actively pursuing this for yourself?
- When you're under stress, how do you calm down?
- What is your favorite human quality?
- Do you have any dreams you have not yet achieved? If so, why not?
- What do you want written on your tombstone?
- What are your fears? How do you deal with them?

- What type of relationship do you have with your family?
- How often do you talk with your parents? Your siblings?

Be sure that you are using the SpeedDating techniques we discussed in Questions 12 and 13. These techniques include relying on your date's actions in addition to words to avoid jumping to inaccurate conclusions.

By the end of the first month or so, you should have a good first impression of your date. During the second month you'll gather more information, which will either confirm your initial evaluation or disprove it.

revealing yourself

Sharing who you are with another person also requires a plan. Some people rush to tell their date too much about themselves during their first meeting, while others are so reserved or war-torn from previous bad dates that they hesitate to show who they really are.

If you struggle with revealing yourself—either you feel you rush too quickly or are too reserved—try using a technique based on the chart:

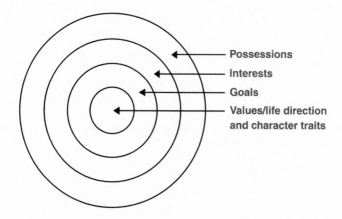

Before each date, think about what you are going to share about yourself with your date based on this chart. During the first month, you may feel very comfortable talking about your possessions and interests, and you might feel comfortable talking about a few goals. But it is the rare person to whom you want to expose your innermost self in the first few dates.

Remember that if someone asks you a question you don't feel comfortable answering, you have the right to simply say that you don't feel comfortable answering that question quite yet.

question 16

did my date pass the team screen?

 Ideally you've been in contact with your team throughout the dating process. If not, at the end of the first month, be sure to contact your date coach and anyone else on your team whose opinion you want.

At this stage, we recommend that you and your team screen your date to see if he passes the "team screen." This is essentially a list of the deal breakers/deal makers you developed and decided upon in Part 1.

Below is a sample screen prepared by Karin, a SpeedDater. Karin is a thirty-two-year-old artist looking for a committed relationship. With her team, Karin will evaluate Kevin, her date, against the screen.

sample screen—deal-maker/ deal-breaker list

Question	Ideal	My Date
1. The four character traits I want in a relationship.	• A positive attitude • Responsiblility (i.e., financial) • Focus on commitment/loyalty • A giving nature	Kevin's actions have demonstrated that he has a positive attitude and a giving nature. I don't know him well enough to know if he is commitment-focused and responsible. I'll be exploring these in the next month.
2. External circumstances I would like.	• Intelligent • Physically fit • Educated (college or equivalent) • Established in career (or preparing for one)	Kevin is intelligent and establishing a career as a banker. He isn't so involved in exercise—which is okay with me.
3. My direction in life, goals, and values.	I want to balance a family and career with the focus on family. As a graphic designer I believe I can find a good balance. Art is very important to me and I would like to find someone who appreciates my artistic nature and career direction as well as shares my desire to build a family.	Kevin is not artistic—but he loves that I am. He enjoys hearing about and seeing my work. He too wants a family. We have similar directions in life.

Question	Ideal	My Date
4. Interests and values I would like us to share.	Deal breaker: he must believe in God and be willing to raise our children with religion. I would love for him to enjoy exercise.	Kevin is definitely spiritual, but we haven't spoken about kids yet. He's not very interested in exercise, but that's okay with me given his other good qualities.
5. How I want to feel when introducing my date to my team and family.	I want to feel proud to be seen with him.	I do feel proud to introduce him to my team. I haven't introduced him to my family yet.
6. Deal-breaking character flaws.	Chronically angry or depressed.	Kevin has a bit of a short temper but is not an angry or depressed person.

Now that you've seen an example, try creating your own:

sample screen

Question	Ideal	My Date
1. The four character traits I want in a relationship.		
2. External circumstances I would like.		
3. My direction in life, goals, and values.		
4. Interests and values I would like us to share.		
5. How I want to feel when introducing my date to my team and family.		
6. Deal-breaking character flaws.		

Let's briefly review each section of the screen:

1. Character Traits

From Question 3 you should have a list of the four top character traits you are looking for in a partner. Share these with your date coach. If you believe your date has these qualities, explain to your date coach your date's specific actions that demonstrates the qualities.

Remember Jennifer from Question 3? She was looking for someone with a strong sense of responsibility, sensitivity, a positive attitude, and loyalty (willingness to commit to a long-term relationship). Within a couple of months of dating, Jennifer was confident that Paul possessed these qualities. She knew this because she focused on his actions and how he responded to certain questions she asked.

At the time she met Paul, he was struggling financially and was in a bit of debt. But Jennifer was not worried about his sense of responsibility. Paul had graduated from a demanding college and had paid most of the tuition himself. In addition, he had a plan for his career, and he was executing it. His positive attitude emerged in many situations—such as how he rebounded from upsets.

Regarding the characteristic of loyalty, Jennifer noticed how committed Paul was to his family. He genuinely cared about his parents and grandparents. He visited and called them regularly, and he spoke about them respectfully. Around the end of their first month of dating, Jennifer told Paul she was looking for a committed relationship and wouldn't waste time in something not headed in that direction. Paul was not intimidated by this; in fact, he was attracted to Jennifer's directness and strength of character.

2. External Circumstances

In answering Question 3 you also developed a list of the external circumstances you are looking for in a partner. If you are artistically inclined, you might want to find someone similar, or at least someone who respects and admires art. If you value physical fitness, you may want to find someone who enjoys exercise and is physically fit.

Remember Alison from Question 9? She was looking for someone who either had a career or was preparing for one. Despite the fact that Steve's external situation indicated that he was not about to settle into a career anytime soon, she continued to date him. This in itself might not have been a huge barrier to the relationship, but he also demonstrated no signs of responsibility—a key character trait for Alison. By reviewing her screen with her date coach, Alison was able to see this, whereas previously she had been blinded by Steve's good looks and natural charisma.

3 and 4. Direction in Life, Goals, and Values

From Question 4 you should have a sense of your life direction and which aspects are important to share with a partner. Share this with your date coach. Do you and your date appear to be going in the same direction?

Think about the future. If you envision a family, do you and your date have similar views about family, such as religion and schooling for children? Often these issues are minor when you're single or married without children, but become major once children are born. So consider them now and explore them with your date and with your date coach!

5. Introducing Your Date to Your Team

One test of the potential success of a relationship is how you feel introducing your date to your team. If you find yourself making excuses for him or not wanting to introduce him, that usually indicates a problem. You should feel proud to introduce him to your team and proud to be seen with him.

Sam had most of the qualities Stacey was looking for in a partner. He was smart, funny, accomplished, generous, kind, and responsible. However, she found that she felt embarrassed introducing him to her team because he lacked social skills. Stacey had never thought social skills were important to her, but as a result of dating Sam, she discovered that they were— she needed a partner who could handle social situations with greater ease.

6. Deal-Breaking Character Flaws

If you believe that your date is free of flaws and that the relationship is perfect, it's almost certainly a sign that the relationship is not grounded in reality. Imperfection is inherent in all humans—and the only questions are, Can you live with those imperfections? How does your date handle those imperfections? Does she recognize them and actively work on improving them, or does she become defensive and refuse to acknowledge them, let alone work on them?

While everyone will have flaws, it's important to know which ones you could live with and which ones you could not—those are your deal breakers. When Sue was dating, she knew she couldn't handle someone with low or negative energy. Yaacov knew that he couldn't live with an excessively needy or dependent person.

It is a sign of great character when a person has actively worked on improving a character trait. On a date with Paula, Mitchell was very impressed when Paula mentioned that she used to be very lazy, but that she had worked on this trait and was now quite productive. It wasn't so much that Paula had become less lazy, but that she had identified a negative quality within herself and had actively worked to improve it, that impressed Mitchell. This indicated to Mitchell that Paula's willingness to work on herself was strong.

By the end of the first month, you may not be able to answer all of these points about your date definitively, but you should be getting a clear sense of who your date really is. In the second month, as you continue to learn, you can continue to use the screen as the relationship progresses.

We should say here that the team screen is meant as a guide to keep you grounded; it is not meant to be cast in stone. You may meet someone who has three out of the four qualities you are looking for—and you may still want to pursue the relationship. Or you might learn that certain qualities are more important to you than others—and modify your screen. It is a warning sign, however, if you continue dating someone who meets only a few of your requirements.

By using the screen as a guide and by communicating with your team, you'll maximize your chances of getting to know who your date truly is, in a relatively short amount of time. In the next Question, we explore other techniques besides just talking with your date that will help you better get to know him.

q u e s t i o n   1 7

how does my date behave when *not* on a date?

 A key to the speed of SpeedDating is discovering who your date is when he's not on a "date"—and the second month of dating is usually a good time to start. From a Jewish perspective, a person does not get big points for exhibiting good character traits around someone he wants to impress (i.e., his date!). It is a sign of greatness when a person *consistently* acts impressively—even around people he may not need to impress, like a waiter, the cabdriver, and certain relatives.

It is extremely important to get to know your date outside of the typical dating scenarios because a lifelong, committed relationship is more than one long date. A committed relationship means seeing each other at all times of the day and night in all types of moods and situations.

Many singles erroneously believe they need to live with a person before they make a commitment in order to see all the different facets of their partner's personality, or at least spend a long time in the evaluation process. We find that living together or any overly lengthy evaluation period causes couples to become deeply enmeshed in each other's lives and makes a breakup, if it happens, even more painful—or couples "settle" for each other to avoid the pain of breaking up.

The evaluation process can be shortened significantly by using certain tools to determine your date's true character. Let's explore these tools.

ciso caso coso: money, anger, alcohol

In Jewish tradition a key to accurately evaluate another person involves a phrase: "Ciso caso coso." This translates idiomatically to: notice how she spends her money, how she handles her anger, and how she handles her liquor (or acts when extremely tired).

Ciso—How a Person Spends Money

The state of a person's checkbook (or credit card history) is a great insight into his character, because how a person spends money and what he spends his money on reflects his true values.

During the first month of dating, Samantha noticed that her date, Jon, always left a large tip for the server—upward of 20–25 percent. Initially, she did not know if this reflected generosity or an irresponsibility toward finances. During her second month of dating Jon, she asked him why he left much more than the standard 15 percent. Jon's answer was very revealing. In high school he had been a waiter, and he has had empathy toward people who wait on him ever since.

Liz noticed that Barry seemed to buy every new electronic gadget available. He also lived in a very expensive apartment building with a pool, exercise room, sauna, and Jacuzzi. During their second month of dating Liz casually asked him one day if he had a 401(k) or other savings plan. "No, I haven't really started saving yet—I can't afford it," he replied. Liz became concerned that Barry was the type of person who would spend most of what he earned, whereas she liked to save a percentage of her income each month.

Liz didn't jump to this conclusion from this one conversation, but she identified finances as an area of potential concern that needed further exploration. As she got to know Barry better, she expressed her concern about his view of finances. When he became defensive, she realized their relationship probably wouldn't work out. Had he been at least open to hearing a different perspective about money, she would have been encouraged that they might find a middle ground on their divergent views.

Caso—How a Person Handles Anger

It is important to notice what makes your date angry and how he expresses it.

Tim had always been very considerate to Tina on their dates, but she noticed that he was very impatient with other people, such as restaurant servers, box office attendants, and store clerks. He would become irritated about minor delays or miscommunications and begin to degrade the "offender." This alerted Tina to pay attention to how Tim treated his parents and others close to him. She noticed that when he spoke with his mother, he often became annoyed. This concerned Tina, and she wondered when she, too, would begin to irritate Tim. In their second month of dating, Tina decided to ask Tim about his short temper; given what she had witnessed so far, she was considering breaking up with him. In a nonthreatening way she mentioned to Tim that he seemed to become easily annoyed with others, including his mother. She was encouraged when Tim didn't become defensive. He admitted that a short temper was one of his flaws, but that he had been actively working on it for years and was today much more patient than in the past! Tim's willingness to work on this problem was impressive to

Tina, and she continued to date him, realizing that no one is perfect, but those people who have a product development (self-improvement) muscle are much easier to live with than those who do not.

Coso—How a Person Handles Alcohol (or Fatigue)

Let us be very clear: we are not recommending that you go out and get drunk with your date! However, seeing how a person handles alcohol can be very revealing. There is a saying in Judaism, "Enter wine, exit secrets!" We hope you will not see your date intoxicated—but do notice how he relates to and handles alcohol.

Also notice how your date behaves when tired. In a committed relationship, especially if children come along, you will often see your partner when he is very tired. You'll be seeing your partner early in the morning and after a hard day at work. Carolyn, a SpeedDater, would ask her dates to meet her at eight on Sunday mornings at a café to see what they were like early in the day!

the unexpected visit

Another way to get a glimpse of who your date really is, is to pay an unexpected visit to your date's workplace. Find a time when you know your visit won't be unduly intrusive, when there will be other people around, and don't plan to stay for very long—just long enough to drop off a small gift or say "hello."

While there, notice how your date interacts with other people and how they treat him. Cindy, a SpeedDater, had been dating Jerry for about six weeks. He had passed her screen, and they really enjoyed being together. At about this point, Cindy felt comfortable paying an unexpected visit to Jerry's office. Jerry was a business consultant at a prestigious firm. On the day of the visit she walked into the foyer, and the receptionist, recognizing her, motioned for her to go back to Jerry's office. When she stepped into the hallway, she heard screaming and yelling from his office. As she approached his door, she realized Jerry was the one yelling! He was berating someone on the phone. She stood outside his office for a few minutes, waiting for his phone call to end. A secretary walked by and smiled at her. "He has a temper, doesn't he?" she said knowingly.

Cindy was stunned. She had never seen this side of Jerry. He had always acted so calm and polite on dates. He had never raised his voice.

When Jerry hung up the phone, Cindy knocked tentatively on the door. Jerry was glad to see her. Cindy simply said, "I was in the neighborhood and wanted to say hi, but I don't want to disturb you!" and shortly thereafter left.

Now, being a SpeedDater, Cindy did not jump to conclusions about what the screaming episode signified. It was another piece of the puzzle—but a very important piece. She asked him about the incident during their next date. Jerry smiled and said his yelling was an act; he wasn't really angry, but he used his loud voice as a negotiating tactic.

Again, Cindy didn't rush to believe or disbelieve him. She simply acknowledged to herself that maybe Jerry had a temper, or maybe, as he explained, he just pretended to be angry in certain work-related scenarios. Either way, she knew she would need more information about this character trait of Jerry's. She decided to use another SpeedDating technique, "the Test."

the test

When we teach this technique, people typically don't like the idea of it at first. But it is extremely effective, so we are going to share it with you. The Test is exactly that: you set up an uncomfortable situation and then observe how your date responds.

Cindy decided to observe how Jerry would act when she made a mistake that inconvenienced him. She and Jerry planned to have dinner at a popular restaurant. Cindy told Jerry to meet her there at 7:00 P.M., but she had actually made dinner reservations for 7:30 P.M. Cindy made sure to arrive at the restaurant early to greet Jerry. When he came in, tired and hungry from a long day at work, she approached him and said, "I'm so sorry, I made a mistake. The reservation is at 7:30 P.M., and they are totally booked; they can't take us sooner."

Jerry looked incredulous. "You made the reservation for the wrong time?" he asked, beginning to raise his voice and embarrassing Cindy a bit. "Well, I guess so," answered Cindy. Jerry, struggling to keep his temper in check, turned away from Cindy to find a place to sit down and wait.

The volatility of Jerry's response made Cindy believe that he did have a temper problem—first she had heard him ranting at work, and then a simple thirty-minute delay had evoked an angry response. Cindy broke up with Jerry. They had been dating for only six weeks, a total of nine dates. She was able to glean the information she needed about Jerry and the relationship in nine dates, compared to the nine months it might have taken a non-SpeedDater!

Cindy continued to use this test on other dates who passed her screen. One date, Matthew, upon hearing Cindy's mistake, smiled and said cheerfully, "That's good news! It will give us time to get a drink at the bar and talk some more." Cindy and Matthew eventually become engaged after five months of dating, but it wasn't this test that was the deciding factor.

meeting family and friends

After Cindy and Matthew had been dating for four months, Matthew sat down with Cindy and told her he truly believed their relationship had a future. "I agree," said Cindy, "but I haven't met your family yet." For Cindy, meeting Matthew's family was a critical piece of the puzzle she needed to see before committing to the relationship. In fact, one deal breaker on her screen was a date's communication with his family.

As discussed in Question 13, SpeedDaters make sure that what their date tells them is proven by actions. Matthew had spoken in glowing terms about his relationship with his parents, but not until Cindy saw the relationship in action was she going to draw a conclusion about Matthew's family dynamic. When Matthew first spoke of his family, Cindy thought, "Matthew *says* he has a close relationship with his family—but until I see how he acts with his parents or how he treats them, I won't know what 'close' means to him." This doesn't mean that Cindy didn't believe what Matthew was saying; she simply wanted to see whether his actions were consistent with his words.

Once she met Matthew's family, Cindy was able to see that Matthew's talk of his close family relationships matched her vision of a close family. Shortly afterward they became engaged.

There is another reason to get to know your date's family and/or close friends: they can be great sources of information about your date. You can ask them to tell you stories about your date, perhaps of when he was a child, or how he got his first job. Such stories often reveal insights into a person's character.

Be careful choosing who you ask and ask questions tactfully to ensure that you obtain the information without being offensive.

When Sue and Yaacov were dating, Sue approached a mutual friend of theirs and asked if she could come over and talk one evening. Sue chose this friend because she trusted his opinion and his judgment. During that evening Sue asked the mutual friend what he admired about Yaacov, what he thought Yaacov's weak points might be, and other similar questions. From this, Sue confirmed that many of the good qualities she saw in Yaacov were seen by others, and she also received some input regarding his weak points.

introduce your date to your team

As we noted in Question 16, a final tool for evaluating your date is to introduce your date to your date coach and anyone else on your team you think would be beneficial. Notice how you feel introducing your date to your team—are you proud, embarrassed, awkward? Your team's evaluation of your date should be a critical component of your evaluation. Note that your date does not have to know that this is your "team."

question 1 8

what challenges will this relation- ship have, and am i prepared to handle or live with these challenges long-term?

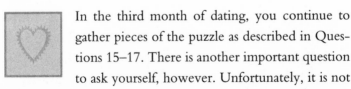 In the third month of dating, you continue to gather pieces of the puzzle as described in Questions 15–17. There is another important question to ask yourself, however. Unfortunately, it is not a question daters typically want to think about. The question, simply put, is: What challenges are present in this relationship,

and what challenges do you foresee for the future? The importance of this question cannot be overemphasized. When a couple begins dating, both people are often carried away by their feelings of connection and by all the positive qualities they have found in each other. In their euphoria, they are likely to overlook or gloss over any lurking problems, or they may only focus on the current problems and not consider problems that may arise in the future, such as differences of opinion about how to raise children, for example.

Early in a relationship it is important to be thinking about the challenges of the relationship because all relationships have challenges. In fact, if you're dating someone and can't think of any challenges the relationship has or might face in the future, you are almost certainly living in a fantasy that will eventually evaporate.

Carla had been dating Stephen for six weeks and was absolutely swept away by their connection. "I think I've found the One! We talk about everything and have such a great connection," she told Yaacov. Yaacov began to ask her questions about Stephen. She told him that Stephen was thirty-nine years old, never married, and had been orphaned at age eleven. "Don't you think that the fact that Stephen is thirty-nine, orphaned, and not married may possibly raise a red flag?" Yaacov asked. Being thirty-nine and never married doesn't automatically mean a person has a problem with commitment, but it should be considered. In addition, being orphaned at eleven is extremely traumatic. Yet, when Yaacov mentioned both of these points, Carla brushed them aside. "Everyone has wounds," she responded. Carla was not willing to admit that some wounds run deeper than others.

Within a couple of weeks Carla called Yaacov with concerns. "Stephen is having a hard time as we're becoming closer," she confided. As it turned out, Stephen was unable to handle their deepening feelings of emotional intimacy and asked Carla to slow down the relationship. Not long thereafter, Carla realized that Stephen would be unable to achieve a deep level of commitment without help from a therapist. That meant it would be a while before he could commit to anyone, let alone her. Now, Carla had a choice. She could either choose to remain with Stephen during this time and deal with the challenge of not knowing if Stephen would ever be able to make a commitment. Or she could choose not to accept this challenge and move on to find another, more promising relationship. She chose the latter.

choose your challenge

It's essential to think about the challenges of a relationship because once you do, you then have the luxury of choosing some of your challenges consciously, at least where it comes to your relationship. It is perfectly okay to choose to accept a difficult challenge—as long as you are doing it willingly and realistically. Otherwise, resentments can build that may lead to dis-illusionment and an eventual painful breakup.

When we (Yaacov and Sue) were dating, it was very easy for us to identify one of the long-term challenges we would face together. We had vastly different views on how to handle finances. Yaacov is, shall we say, idealistic and has a strong belief that he will always have what he needs. Based on this view, he would feel comfortable living without life insurance or retirement savings.

Sue, on the other hand, is more concerned than Yaacov about family finances and security. She believes it's a responsibility to save for retirement and hold life insurance. When Sue considered this challenge to their long-term relationship, she decided that she could not comfortably live within Yaacov's financial vision. Sue decided that as long as Yaacov was not against savings and life insurance, then she would live with the challenge of differing views by supplementing the family income if necessary. Yaacov was open to this lifestyle and now includes savings for retirement and life insurance in our family budget.

Studies show that when most couples fight, they fight about money. We confronted a very important long-term challenge in our relationship before we married. After our discussion we both thought things over and then made a conscious decision that we could live with this challenge through mutual compromise and, thus, with each other.

future challenges

Future challenges typically involve how couples feel about money, children, family, and religion. If a couple is not in accord on these issues, there may be great tension in the relationship, especially once children are involved.

Case in point: Kurt and Lynda had been dating for over three months when they learned the principles of SpeedDating. They applied the principles and began asking each other questions about the future, such as:

- Do you want children?
- Ideally, how many children would you want?
- In what, if any, religion do you want to bring up the children?
- What are your views on education? Would you want to send the children to public, private, or parochial schools?
- How do you want to spend the holidays and/or vacations? With relatives? Alone? A combination?
- How involved do you envision our families being in our lives now and when we have children?
- How would you envision our household running—how would household chores be divided up?

As Kyle and Lynda discussed these questions, they realized they had significant differences. Kyle wanted to have at least three or four children. Lynda couldn't imagine having more than two. Kyle wanted to send his children to religious day schools, whereas Lynda was unsure of this plan. Kyle and Lynda did decide to get married, yet they did so with a clear understanding of their differences. Kyle was willing to compromise and only have two children; Lynda was willing to compromise and send them to a religious day school. To this day Kyle wishes he had more than two children, but he respects the commitment he made to Lynda. More importantly, he understood before marrying her that this disappointment would both exist and be a challenge for him and that he could handle it. Similarly, Lynda felt uncomfortable sending her children to religious day school, but honored her commitment to Kyle regardless of her personal feelings. This would be a challenge for her, but one that she consciously chose ahead of time. The key to their successful marriage is that they both went into the relationship understanding the challenges, and thus would not hold resentments against each other.

what are my date's character flaws?

Your date, like any human, will have character flaws. Can you live with those character flaws?

Brad and Brenda were seriously considering marriage, but

Brad had a strong concern about Brenda's disorganization. Brad was a "neat freak." It drove him crazy to see her cluttered car, and he found himself cleaning up after Brenda when they were dating.

The good news is that Brad was aware of the challenge. The question he had to ask himself was, Can I live with Brenda's messiness long-term? Brad decided he could not. When he confided this to Brenda, however, she committed to ensuring that they would have cleaning help, even if it meant spending less on vacations or eating out. Today Brenda and Brad are married, and even though they don't yet have children, they have cleaning help twice a week!

the importance of listening

Listening with the goal of understanding is critical to successful SpeedDating. This type of listening, sometimes called active listening, or empathetic listening, allows you to make sure you completely understand what your date is saying and not put your own "spin" on your date's words or actions. This technique is especially helpful when discussing challenges or potential future challenges.

Active listening can be used with family, friends, and colleagues to prevent misunderstandings. It allows you to verify exactly what someone else is saying, thus avoiding misinterpretations. It is easy to practice. One technique is as follows: after someone has finished telling you something, simply repeat what they said to you *in your own words* after beginning with something like, "What I hear you saying is . . ." Then repeat what you think you heard. At that point, the person can either confirm that what you heard was accurate or correct any misunderstandings. With this technique, both parties end up on the same wavelength about the conversation.

Wrong:

Kitty: A close family is important to me. I like being near my folks.

Bob: *(Jumping to conclusions.)* So you won't move away from New York?

Kitty: *(Feeling defensive.)* I didn't say that—but maybe I wouldn't.

Right:

Kitty: A close family is important to me. I like being near my folks.

Bob: What I hear you saying is that you wouldn't want to leave New York.

Kitty: Not necessarily, but I'd want to be able to visit my family often.

Imagine the arguments you can avoid simply by using active listening and clarifying what your date is saying!

A key to empathetic listening is focusing your attention on understanding what the other person is saying, versus expressing your own opinion. For example:

Wrong

Rick: I love going to the shooting range to practice using my gun.

Michelle: *(Stating her opinion.)* You know, guns are so dangerous, I would never have one in my house.

Rick: *(Feeling defensive and stating his opinion.)* They don't have to be dangerous if you know what you're doing.

Michelle: *(Stating her opinion with the goal of proving him wrong.)* Of course guns are dangerous—even if you know what you're doing, your child or a burglar might find the gun. No, owning a gun is terrible.

Right

Rick: I love going to the shooting range to practice using my gun.

Michelle: *(Seeking to understand.)* You find it fun?

Rick: Fun? Yes, fun—but it reminds me of my father—he used to take me shooting when we lived in Kentucky. He passed away a few years ago, so every once in a while I just take my gun to the range and remember what he taught me.

Michelle: *(Seeking to understand.)* Wow, so the gun is very meaningful to you.

Rick: Yes—it's funny. I don't even keep bullets at home—I just buy them at the range and use them there. Guns can be dangerous if you don't know what you're doing or if they fall into the wrong hands.

Michelle: I totally agree—guns can be dangerous.

In the "right" example, Michelle temporarily suspends her own opinion while focusing on understanding Rick's point of view. This kind of listening opens people up and enables them to share themselves with another. Empathetic listening helps you get to know your date without misjudging him. It is especially useful when talking about sensitive, challenging topics.

Being able to talk honestly and constructively about challenges is a good indication of the potential success of your relationship. So, when considering the potential of a particular date, ask yourself the following questions:

- Am I able to easily bring up sensitive issues?
- When I bring up these issues, does my date become defensive or shut down?
- Do my date and I actively listen not only to hear but to understand what the other is saying?

awareness of challenges can be a positive sign

Dalia came to visit Sue because she was concerned about her relationship with Evan. They had been dating for over three months. "I know what one of our challenges would be," Dalia began. "As a teacher he doesn't make a lot of money, and I can be really materialistic. So if I marry Evan, I would need to let go of that part of me—but it's a part of me I don't like anyway. Still, it's hard to let go. And Evan finds me challenging as well because I push him to live by his true priorities in order to reach his goals, which is one of the reasons he respects me so much."

What Dalia was saying is actually beautiful. She had found someone who pushed her to be a better person, and vice versa. Overcoming challenges like Dalia's and Evan's bring a couple closer together because they help each other grow. This shared growth is the essence of the thoughtful giving we discussed in Question 5 because each person in the relationship is enabling the other to reach his potential.

a word about commitment

As discussed in Question 6, singles (often women) complain that their dates (i.e., men!) want to avoid commitment. There are two things we have to say about this. First, there are many people, including many men, who are interested in commitment! Using the SpeedDating principles will help you weed out the noncommitters relatively quickly, so you are open and available to meeting someone who is seeking a lifelong relationship.

Secondly, we suggest that you make it a priority to discuss where your date stands on the issue of commitment relatively early. It's impossible for us to tell you exactly when to bring this up because each dating scenario is different, but we can offer some guiding principles. Typically, commitment shouldn't be discussed on the first date or two. Your focus during those dates should simply be on whether you enjoy being with each other.

Discuss with your team when to bring up commitment. Certainly by the third month of consistently dating the same person, this topic should be discussed. It is important to approach it confidently. You should be asking about where he stands on commitment from a position of confidence, not desperation or anger.

Asking for what you need in terms of commitment in a relationship can and does work. Reed and Denise had been dating for about two months when Denise brought up commitment in a very direct manner. "I'm twenty-nine," she told Reed, "and I'm looking to find a long-term relationship. So if in another five months we still aren't sure where the relationship is headed, I will have to break it off." She was not demanding that he be ready for commitment. Instead, she simply was letting him know what she needed and how she anticipated pursuing it. She was honest and clear about her intentions. Reed was impressed with both Denise's confidence and lack of fear of asking for what she needed. Today they are happily married with two baby girls.

What's the lesson here? Simple. Don't avoid asking your date his feelings about commitment for fear of what you'll find out. If you approach your dating goals with confidence, you will simply be weeding out the flakes and impressing the commitment-minded!

Any relationship will have challenges—there's no way around it. By being aware of potential challenges, however, you can have more control over those you bring into your life. Ultimately, this will help ensure a strong, healthy relationship.

SpeedDating Exercise

Answer the questions below:

1. What are the current challenges in your relationship?

2. What could be the future challenges?

3. Are you prepared to handle these challenges? If so, what is your strategy?

4. What are your date's character flaws?

5. Can you live with these flaws? How? Do you have a strategy, as Brad and Brenda did? If not, can you create one you can live with?

is this my soul mate?

By the third or fourth month of SpeedDating you should have a good idea of whether the person you are dating is the right one. But you may have doubts. To help clarify any misgivings you may have, we'd like to conclude with a discussion about soul mates.

There are three questions we hear about soul mates:

- Do soul mates exist?
- How can I recognize my soul mate?
- Could I have missed my soul mate?

do soul mates exist?

Judaism holds that soul mates do exist—but they may appear different from what you imagine. Your soul mate is not Prince or Princess Charming. Nor is your soul mate a perfect person. Your soul mate is the person who will best help you reach your potential, and vice versa.

Your soul mate will certainly be someone who appreciates your values and encourages you to reach your goals. In addition, your soul mate will love you for who you are, and be able to live with or at least tolerate your flaws. Simultaneously you should also appreciate your soul mate's goals and values and actively encourage her to achieve them.

While all this may sound romantic, in reality living with your soul mate can at times be quite aggravating or at least challenging, because becoming the best person you can be can take serious effort.

When we (Yaacov and Sue) were first married, Sue had a habit that drove Yaacov crazy. Sue would leave her half-filled teacups around the apartment, instead of bringing them into the kitchen. Sue didn't see what the big deal was—she could always bring the cups in later. But Yaacov felt uncomfortable living with that level of disorganization.

On a spiritual level, this was a perfect situation for us. It gave Sue the "opportunity" to thoughtfully give to Yaacov and increase her sensitivity toward him. And it gave Yaacov the opportunity to work on his patience as Sue slowly changed her habit. This difference in our living styles enabled us both to grow; Sue became more sensitive to her husband's needs, and Yaacov became more patient.

how can i recognize my soul mate?

One of the most important actions you can take to be sure you recognize your soul mate is to be true to yourself—to your values and goals. If you are aware of who you are and what you are looking for, you'll be better prepared to recognize the right person when you meet her. We hope this book has helped you achieve this clarity through focusing on your direction in life, your priorities, and the character traits you admire.

Below is a Soul Mate Checklist to help you recognize your soul mate. Notice how it mirrors what we've been discussing about SpeedDating throughout this book.

Soul Mate Checklist:

1. I can list four character traits of my partner that I respect and admire, and he/she can articulate character traits he/she respects about me.

2. I appreciate and support my partner's values. And my partner appreciates and supports mine.
3. I can see myself actively helping my partner achieve his/her goals, or at least being supportive of them, and my partner does this for me.
4. We've discussed some challenges we face or may face in our relationship and are prepared to work through or live with those challenges.
5. I know of at least one of my partner's character flaws, and I'm prepared to live with the flaw(s).
6. I feel attracted to my partner, and my partner feels attracted to me.
7. I have actively worked on an aspect of my character to improve myself—and my partner has demonstrated his or her ability and desire to work on him/herself.

have i missed my soul mate?

One of the greatest fears we hear from singles, especially women, is that they have missed their soul mate. However, if you are being true to yourself, through being honest about your values and goals as discussed in previous chapters, you stand the best chance of finding your lifelong partner.

If you have not been true to yourself in the past, or if you have made major changes in your life, you can still find your soul mate. It is a traditional Jewish belief that at any given time there are a handful of people who could be your soul mate. The choices you make determine which of those people can emerge in your life as the right one. Typically, the clearer you are about who you are and the type of person you are looking for, the easier it will be for you to find your soul mate.

Remember Nina, from Question 4. Nina did not clarify what she wanted in life until her thirties. Once she decided the type of life she wanted to lead and the type of person with whom she wanted to share it, then—and only then—was she able to recognize her soul mate.

Sometimes we meet singles who are so desperate to get married, or so lonely, that they try to mold themselves into what they believe another person will want. Ironically, for the reasons we've discussed, this doesn't help; in fact it hurts their chances of finding and recognizing the right person.

No matter what your circumstances, if you are committed to being true to yourself, and following the SpeedDating path, you are creating the best possible chance of meeting your soul mate.

We encourage you to continue on your journey, and we hope this book will be part of your permanent SpeedDating team.

afterword

The People of the Book have always maintained that there is the intelligent way to do everything. That there is the intelligent way to live, the intelligent way to work, the intelligent way to eat, the intelligent way to spend, the intelligent way to love, and even the intelligent way to disagree.

Yaacov and Sue Deyo—a highly intelligent and creative couple I have had the privilege of knowing and respecting even longer than they've known each other—make available to the public attitudes and techniques for dating intelligently, based on age-old concepts and years of experience in helping people find direction in life. *SpeedDating* offers the reader a framework for avoiding years of unintelligent dating that often culminate in failed or unhealthy relationships and despair. Written in a straightforward and uncomplicated manner, *SpeedDating* is a user-friendly guide to simplifying the complex process of finding a partner for life.

—Rabbi Yitzchak Berkovits

appendix a:

secrets to successful seven-minute dating

 SpeedDating events are a new way to meet people. At first experience its newness expresses itself in terms of its speed! Participants meet for seven minutes in an efficient format of round-robin dating. At a seven-minute dating event, you can determine who are likely candidates for a relationship more quickly than you can by milling about at parties.

Another aspect of the program's newness is its sensitivity. This may seem surprising: How can an efficient system of dating, in which people are processed through short dates, be sensitive as well?

We believe it can, and we've worked in subtle rules to help ensure that the SpeedDating experience is an enjoyable one, whether or not participants meet others they would like to date again. We've looked carefully at contemporary dating behavior and layered a number of timeless principles of Jewish wisdom into our SpeedDating rules. In the next few paragraphs, we would like to outline these rules and the value each adds to the experience.

Rule #1: You may not ask where your date lives or what he/she does for a living.

We believe that character issues comprise a large part of relationships. Therefore, determining a person's true character is the due diligence of dating. You may be a rocket scientist, but SpeedDaters want to know if you're a good person.

In addition, many people love to talk about their work. Our lives can be dominated by such conversations. If you do not ask this question, it has been our experience, the conversations are more fresh and real. Try it, and you'll see!

Rule #2: Do not let any of your dates know whether or not you chose them.

Each participant is given a dating card with seven boxes in which to make notes about each of that evening's seven dates. After each date, you indicate on the card whether you would like to see that person again for a longer, more traditional date. If both participants indicate that they would like to date each other again, it is a mutual match. We call each person the next day, and give each the other's phone number. As you fill out the card, please make an effort not to let the other person see your choices. As we all know, rejection can be very painful. We're here to mute the rejection a little by providing an indirect process of letting the other person know. This is a timely, respectful, and indirect way to bring closure to the date. It also makes the dates themselves more fun and less stressful.

Rule #3: Men move, and women stay seated.

In describing aspects of courtship, the Talmud relates that it is the way of men to chase women. We've designed this gender inclination into SpeedDating to help make the events more comfortable for participants.

Once all the preregistered participants have arrived at the coffeehouse and been issued a name tag and table number, we ask the women to sit at the tables corresponding to their number. The women stay at these tables for the remainder of the evening. At the sound of a bell, each of the men sit at the table corresponding to their number and begin dating the women seated with them. After seven minutes, we ring the bell again, and then ask all participants to fill out their dating cards for the date they just finished. We then ask all the men to move to a table two numbers higher than the one at which they were sitting, and begin dating the woman who is seated there. This process is repeated five more times until everyone has dated seven people.

Rule #4: The next table is positioned out of direct line of sight.

You may have had the experience at a party or bar of having someone look over your shoulder and scan the crowd while speaking with you. This is just plain rude! If you're speaking with me, please direct your attention to me! I'm not a social prop like a drink! I'm a person! At SpeedDating events, we set up the room to ensure that dates cannot see directly the next person they will be dating a few tables over. In addition, we ask organizers to have participants conceal their name tags until just before we start the dating.

Rule #5: Answer the question: Was this person polite and respectful?

There are few dating experiences more hurtful than being "written off" before any conversation or exchange has taken place. Imagine being in the company of someone whose speech and body language clearly indicate that you are no longer a prospect. It's awful! We've discouraged this type of behavior in SpeedDating by asking participants to indicate on the dating cards after each date whether or not the person was polite and respectful. In other words, did they use the seven minutes to try and get to know you? If you were "written off," please indicate this. If a participant receives two "no" answers to that question from that night's group of seven dates, he is not invited back.

Rule #6: Indicate immediately after each date whether you would like to see this person again.

One of the unfortunate characteristics of today's dating scene is its lack of purpose and closure. We believe that typical daters keep several people "on the string" either because they do not want to limit their options or because they lack an effective process of getting the clarity they need for closure. For instance, Dan may not want to commit to Cindy because Carolyn might want to go out, and Caitlin looks pretty. Chances are Dan will not get the clarity he needs about any of them while considering all of them.

In SpeedDating, participants spend seven minutes with another person, and are immediately asked for closure: Do you want to date this person again—yes or no? The decision represents the smallest quanta of commitment many men will feel at ease making: yes, I would like to see her again.

Rule #7: No skipping of dates.

By now, if the reason for this rule were not apparent, then we would like to apologize. We have done a poor job of communicating the sensitivities of the program! It would represent truly woeful behavior for a participant to "write off" another by skipping that person's table, leaving her to sit there alone in a room full of others who are dating.

Rule #8: Only seven dates.

Often participants ask that we let everybody date everybody! It's an ambitious desire! We have eschewed this because we believe it's important for us to take responsibility for everyone's experience at SpeedDating. For instance, let's say Mr. Special, Jonathan, dates fifteen or twenty women. Wow! He's thrilled at the opportunity to meet so many people, and it's likely he'll meet someone (or several someones!) he would like to date again. Imagine, however, Howard's experience at the same event. He dates twenty, chooses twelve he would like to see again, and not one of the twelve picks him! He would be devastated! In facilitating Jonathan's dream evening, we've given Howard a very different experience.

By allowing only seven dates, the chances of such hurt feelings are greatly reduced. None of the seven I dated was a mutual match, Harold will imagine, but there were many others there I might have dated. I think I'll come back.

Rule #9: Do not exchange phone numbers.

One of the stressful aspects of dating is the directness of it: Will
he ask for my number or not? Will she give her number to me
or not? Wouldn't it be nice to just have a conversation, and
then worry about the phone number stuff later? We agree.

Rule #10: Have fun!

For more information about SpeedDating visit www.speeddating.com.

appendix b

how to approach seven-minute, round-robin dating and questions to ask on a seven-minute date

 Seven-minute, round-robin dating is a bit different from the classic first date. The obvious difference is in length: it only lasts seven minutes. That means it's important to use the time wisely. Another difference is that, at seven-minute dating events, people typically expect to be asked questions as a way of getting to know each other quickly—so the types of questions can be more probing than those asked during a classic first date. Below is a list of questions we have recommended daters ask at such events. Notice that many of the questions extend beyond interests to goals and values.

The goal of the seven-minute date is similar to that of the first date we discussed in Question 11. In seven minutes, do not expect to know if you have met Mr. or Ms. Right. How-

ever, you can know if you have *not* met the right one! At the
end of a seven-minute date, as you do on a classic first date,
simply ask yourself if you enjoyed talking with the person.
Intense chemistry may or may not be present. As we discussed
throughout this book, chemistry does not always manifest on
the first few dates—and certainly not always in the first seven
minutes—but you should feel interest and curiosity to know
more about the person and a basic sense of connection.

Sample questions to ask on a seven-minute date:

- Did you ever own a pet? What was its name? Why?
- What is the most beautiful place you visited?
- Where are you planning to go on your next vacation?
- What is your favorite musical instrument?
- What's the nicest thing someone did for you this week?
- What are you most appreciative of this week?
- What meaningful event recently occurred in your life?
- Have you ever done any volunteer work? If so, what type?
- What in life would you most like to accomplish?
- When you are under stress, how do you calm down?
- What do you do to stay happy?
- What is your favorite book? Why?
- What is your favorite movie? Why?
- What would you like written on your tombstone?
- Where do you see yourself in five years?

bibliographic essay

The majority of the ideas in this book are based on traditional Jewish wisdom passed from generation to generation for thousands of years. Most of the citations below indicate selected sources of the transmission of these ideas. We would like to thank Rebbetzin Tziporah Heller for helping us locate and/or verify many of the sources.

Question 1: What Is My Desired Outcome?

Kohelet (Ecclesiastes) written by King Solomon, 2:14. "A wise man's eyes are in his head." This is translated in the Midrash to mean that the wise person can envision the future outcomes of his decisions.

Regarding the "Shaper," we source the following:

• Morenu HaRav Lowe (Maharal), *The Maharal's Drash al Torah*, from the midrashic adage in Shmot Rabbah, 22:2. This adage concerns the first sin in the Garden of Eden. Eve is presented as a temptress not because she is evil but because the "woman" has the ability to understand her man and exert influence over him.

• Gemora, Bava Metzia, 59a cf. Ketuvot 67b and Nida 45b, compiled around 300 C.E.

• Tanna Divei Eliahu (an ancient Jewish Midrash). "Who is the able wife? One who does/makes her husband's will." The Hebrew word "does" is the same as the word for "makes" (osa). Some scholars such as Maimonedes understand the word osa in this context to mean "does." Others understand the usage to be incontrovertibly an ambiguous word to mean "makes" as well. In fact, one of today's most well-received books on Jewish marriage that is based on classical sources, *Ohel Rachel*, uses this interpretation as the core of its presentation on Jewish marriage.

Question 2: How Can I Tell When I'm in Love?

We based the ideas of this Question on a work by Rabbi Eliahu Dessler, *Michtav MeEliahu*, vol. 1. This book is a compilation of Rabbi Dessler's essays written in the 1930s and 1940s. In this essay he writes, "There are two sorts of love. One is natural (or in more contemporary language intuitive) and the other is the result of observation and discovery of what is admirable about the one who is beloved. This sort of love is called 'knowledge,' as it says, 'Adam knew his wife.' It is this sort of love that God extends to the righteous." (We have translated this from the Hebrew into English freely rather than literally.)

In addition, these ideas can be found in a work by Rabbi Leibush of Lisa (the Malbim), *Malbim's Commentary on Genesis,* Genesis 24;27. The Malbim lived from 1809–1879.

Rosie Einhorn and Sherry S. Zimmerman wrote *Talking Tachlis* (Southfield, Mich.: Targum/Feldheim, 1998), incorporating many of these ideas.

Menachem Mendel Schneerson (the Rebbe), Adapted by Simon Jacobson, *Toward a Meaningful Life: The Wisdom of the Rebbe* (New York: William Morrow and Company, Inc., 1995), p. 57. Rabbi Schneerson lived from 1902–1994:

- "Love is not the overwhelming, blinding emotion we find in the world of fiction. Real love is an emotion that intensifies throughout life. It is the small, everyday acts of being together that make love flourish. It is sharing and caring and respecting one another. It is building a life together, a family and a home."

Question 3: Am I Attracted to Who People Are, What They Have, or What They Can Do for Me?

For this Question we drew upon two verses from the last book in the Mishna, *Pirkei Avot* (Ethics of the Fathers), compiled around 190 C.E.

- In the 4th Mishna, chap. 27, "Don't look at the flask, but at what is in it. There can be an old flask with recently made wine. There can also be an old flask and it doesn't even contain wine."
- In the 5th Mishna, chap. 19, "Any love that depends on a specific cause, when that cause is gone, the love is gone; but if it does not depend on a specific cause, it will never cease."

Yehuda Lebovits, in his book *Shidduchim and Zivugim* (Southfield, Mich.: Targum Press, 1987) also discusses these ideas.

For the idea that character traits are consistent, we consulted two sources:

- Rabbi Eliahu Dessler's work *Michtav MeEliahu* (Strive for Truth), in the essay: "A Glance at Truth," vol. 1. The essays in *Michtav MeEliahu* were written around the 1930s and 1940s. The English version was translated by Aryeh Carmell (Jerusalem/New York: Feldheim Publishers, 1978).

- In the Dalai Lama's and Howard C. Cutler's book *The Art of Happiness,* p. 21, a study is quoted: "Researchers surveying Illinois state lottery winners and British pool winners, for instance, found that the initial high eventually wore off and the winners returned to their usual range of moment to moment happiness" (New York: Riverhead Books, 1998).

The other works we consulted for this chapter include:

- Menachem Mendel Schneerson (the Rebbe), Adapted by Simon Jacobson, *Toward a Meaningful Life: The Wisdom of the Rebbe* (New York: William Morrow and Company, Inc., 1995), p. 61.
  - "The two types of love—selfish love and selfless love—are diametrically opposed. Selfish love is conditional love; you love on the condition that your needs will be met, and if the person you have chosen to love doesn't serve your needs, you reject that person and search elsewhere. Although it may seem beautiful for a time, such love is bound to be mercurial."
- Victor E. Frankl, *Man's Search for Meaning* (New York: Washington Square Press, 1984), pp. 153–54: "It is not freedom from conditions, but it is freedom to take a stand towards the conditions"; "Man is not fully conditioned and determined but rather determines himself whether he gives in to conditions or stands up to them. In other words man is ultimately self determined."

- Gila Manolson, *The Magic Touch* (New York: Targum/ Feldheim, 1992, 1999).
- Rav Samson Raphael Hirsh, *Commentary on Genesis* 22:2 (New York: Judaica Press, 1971). His commentary on the Torah was published between 1867 and 1878. Rav. Hirsh lived from 1808 to 1888.

Question 4: What Do We Have in Common— and Does It Matter?

Shimon Apisdorf and Nachum Braverman, *Death of Cupid* (Baltimore: Leviathan Press, 1996).

Question 5: What Type of Person Do I Enjoy Giving To?

For the concept of giving and the role it plays in creating and maintaining love, we consulted the following:

- Rabbi Eliahu Dessler's *Michtav MeEliahu*, vol. 1. In the essay "Collected Essays on Loving Kindness," written in the 1930s through 1941. Translated into English by Aryeh Carmell (Jerusalem/New York: Feldheim Publishers, 1978).
- Rav Samson Raphael Hirsh, *Commentary on Genesis* 22:2: "Love requires a glance towards eternity and the

act of giving to solidify and add commitment to love if it is to endure" (New York: Judaica Press, 1971). His commentary on the Torah was published between 1867 and 1878. Rav Hirsh lived from 1808 to 1888.

- Anonymous, *Orchot Tzadekim:* "The soul is infinite and thrives on giving. The body is finite and thrives on taking. Since the body is finite, any pleasure derived from the body will fade. Any pleasure from the soul will last eternally." The date of this work is unknown; it first appeared in 1543.

Question 6: Am I Reliving the Same Bad Date Over and Over Again?

We based many of the concepts of this Question on the following sources from Maimonides and the Steipler Rav, two great Torah luminaries:

- Maimonides (Rambam) in his work the *Mishne Torah,* Sefer HaMada, section *Hilchot Deos.* The Rambam lived between 1135 and 1204.
  - In order to break habits that evolve into negative patterns, we must enact new habits. They must take us (step-by-step) toward the opposite extreme. For instance, an arrogant person must take steps toward authentic humility. If no steps are taken or if the steps taken are not decisive enough,

the person will remain entrapped by the force of
habit.

- While character is formed from a combination of
heredity and environmental issues, it is ultimately
up to the individual to take responsibility for his or
her life circumstances, regardless of the cause. This
is the only way to his happiness and success in finding and making a good life.

- A person enmeshed in bad habits must seek a wise
person for counsel. Not to do so is analogous to not
seeking the help of a doctor for medical issues.

- Steipler Rav in letters written by the Steipler Rav. Cited
in *The Eternal Jewish Home* by Rav Yoel Schwartz. The
Steipler Rav lived from approximately 1897 to 1991.

Question 7: Am I Spending as Much Time in Product Development as I Am in Marketing?

Ideas discussed in this Question can be found in the following
sources:

- Maimonides (Rambam), *Mishna Torah* (1135–1204), vol. 1,
The Book of Knowledge. The Rambam writes that no one is
perfect, but our traits can be channeled to be used for good. It
is this commitment toward channeling existing features of the
character that makes one person righteous (and a good bet for
marriage) and another wicked (and to be avoided).

- John Gray, *Men Are from Mars, Women Are from Venus* (New York: HarperCollins, 1992).

- Rav Eliyahu ben Moshe Vidash in his work *Reishis Chochma*, chapter: *Gate of Fear of God*. "Fear of Sin" written in approximately 1577. Rav Eliayah ben Moshe Vidash lived from approximately 1518 to 1592.

- Vilna Goan, Rabbi Eliahu Kramer, *Evven Shleimah*, with commentary by Rev Chaim of Volvzhin. While the idea of self-change is sourced in the Rambam's *Mishna Torah*, the steps are detailed in *Evven Shleimah*, and Rev Chaim of Volvzhin adds his commentary, which is included in most editions of *Evven Shleimah*.

- Rabbi Eliahu Dessler, *Michtav MeEliahu*. In the subchapter "The potential for evil in the heart." The source of evil is imperfect character traits, which lead to emotional agendas and make knowing the truth a challenge.

Question 8: What Do I Like and Respect about Myself?

- The Torah, Vayikra 19:18.

- Nachmanidies (Ramban) (1194–1270), commentary on Vayikra 19. We do not have the ability to conjure up emotions at will. In fact, even if we were able to do so, the Torah requires that we regard our own lives as our first responsibility. But we must hope for and desire good for others.

• Avraham Twerski, *Let Us Make Man* (Brooklyn, N.Y.: CIS Publication, 1987, 1989, 1991).

• Avraham Twerski, *Like Yourself and Others Will, Too* (Englewood Cliffs, N.J.: Spectrum, 1978).

• Rabbi Nachman of Breslov, *Lekutei Moharan,* originally published in 1808, edited by R' Nassan. Nachman writes, "We all have contact with a deep spiritual need to experience regality. The highest level of attaining a sense of self-worth—genuine regality—comes from removing external trappings of glory from one's own head and restoring them to God." Rabbi Nachman lived from approximately 1771 to 1808.

• Gemarra, *Mesechet Succot* 53.

• Anonymous, *Orchot Tzadekem* (Gate of Arrogance); "An arrogant person will justify mindless seeking of approval and depart from truth."

Question 9: Who Is My Team?

• Shaya Ostrov, *The Inner Circle* (New York: Feldheim, 2000).

- Pirkei Avot, chap. 2, Mishna 8; "Increase council, increase understanding." Compiled around 190 C.E.

- Talmud Bavli, Mesechet Kiddushin 71. Bilaam, the wicked prophet, saw that the doors of the tents that the Jews had set up for their stay in the desert did not face each other (thus offering privacy) and said it is for this reason that the Divine Presence dwells within them. Compiled around 300 C.E.

- Irwin Katsof, *How to Get Your Prayers Answered* (Hollywood, Fla.: Frederick Fell, 2000).

Question 10: Do I Trust That This Is Going to Work Out—That I Will Find My Soul Mate?

- Anonymous, *Orchot Zadekim*. In the essay, "Gate of Happiness." The date of this work is unknown; it was first discovered in 1543.

- Morenu HaRav Lowe (the Maharal). *Netiv HaBitachon*. Chapters 1 and 2 put forth the idea that the merit of having true faith in God and allowing oneself to feel utterly dependent on Him is sufficient for blessing to descend and prayers to be answered. The feeling of authentic happiness is the result of one's trust in God. It is the effect of faith of good things happening. However, happiness in a genuine sense can never be totally removed from faith. It is for this reason that the late

Lubavicher Rebbe was fond of the Yiddish aphorism "tracht goot, s'vett zein goot," which means "think good and it will be good," which is widely quoted in his collected letters.

• Talmud, Sota 42:2. Concerning the verse in Kohelet (Ecclesiastes) 12:25: "A worry in a man's heart should be spoken." Rabbi Ami and Rabbi Assi: one tells us that when a man has a worry he should remove it from his mind, while the other says he should discuss it with others. Compiled around 300 C.E.

Question 12: What Are My Thoughts Telling Me—Which Should I Listen to, and Which Should I Ignore?

• Proverbs 2:2, "Include your heart to wisdom." This tells us that the heart, the seat of emotions, must submit to the mind, the source of rational wisdom.

• Rabbi Eliyahu Dessler, *Strive for Truth*.

• Vilna Goan, *Even Shleimah*, chap. 1.

Question 13: Is This an Action or My Interpretation of an Action?

• Pirkei Avot, chap. 1; "Judge everyone favorably." The technique of suspending judgment is a central pillar of Jewish law.

We are asked to judge favorably when we don't have all the information.

• Maimonides (Rambam), *Sefer Mitzvot*. The Rambam discusses how to judge people. We are obliged to judge ordinary people (neither outstandingly righteous or evil) as meritoriously as the situation merits. This means not jumping to negative conclusions when the situation can just as rationally be seen in a positive light.

• Rabbi Zelig Pliskin, *Patience* (Brooklyn: Artscroll Shaar Press, 2001). "Before judging someone negatively, ask yourself, 'Have I gathered enough data to be certain that my judgement is accurate?'"

• Shimon Apisdorf, Nachum Braverman. *The Death of Cupid* (Leviathan Press, 1996).

Question 14: Is This Relationship Ready for Physical Intimacy?

Menachem Mendel Schneerson (the Rebbe), Adapted by Simon Jacobson, *Toward a Meaningful Life: The Wisdom of the Rebbe* (New York: William Morrow and Company, Inc., 1995), pp. 67, 69, 71. In the chapter "Intimacy," the Rebbe writes in depth about finding true intimacy by correctly channeling physical intimacy.

- "Sexuality is an internal, G-dly energy, a meeting of body and soul, that is nourished by true intimacy. . . . It can only flourish in a healthy manner in the context of the sacred institution of marriage."

- ". . . intimacy is a celebration of vulnerability; it touches the softest spot in each person, the most private and fragile part of a human being. Therefore, we must cultivate a healthy environment for our intimacy, one that allows us to appreciate and revel in this vulnerability, secure and protected."

- Gila Manolson, *The Magic Touch* (New York: Feldheim, 1992/1999).

- Maharal, Gvors Hashem, chap. 24. The Maharal discusses the varying definitions of the word "good."

- Marc and Beth Firestone, www.aish.com, dating section, "Buying without a Test Drive."

Question 17: How Does My Date Behave When *Not* on a Date?

- Pirkei Avot, chap. 2, Mishna 8. It tells us the most essential quality to search for is a good heart, for it incorporates many other good qualities.

- Pirkei Avot, chap. 3.

• Each letter in the Hebrew alphabet represents a numerical value. The numerical value of words often indicates a relationship between words. The study of the numerical value of words is called gematria. For example, regarding the phrase, "enter wine, exit secrets," the gematria of the word "wine" is the same as "secret"—both have the numerical value of 70.

• Eiruvin 65a and b—ciso, caso, coso.

Question 18: What Challenges Will This Relationship Have, and Am I Prepared to Handle or Live with These Challenges Long-term?

On the topic of listening we consulted:

• Pirkei Avot, chap. 6, "Listen with the ear." This teaches that often people erroneously listen with their mouths— formulating their response while the other is talking.

• Stephen R. Covey, *The 7 Habits of Highly Effective People* (New York: Simon & Schuster Fireside, 1990), pp. 235–253.